YOU CAN
READ
ANYONE

YOU CAN
READ
ANYONE

Never Be Fooled, Lied To, or
Taken Advantage Of Again

David J. Lieberman, Ph.D.

Viter Press New Jersey

For information contact:
Viter Press, 1072 Madison Ave., Lakewood, NJ 08701
Email DJLMedia @aol.com Fax 772-619-7828

Publisher's Cataloging-in-Publication

Lieberman, David J.
You can read anyone: never be fooled, lied to, or
taken advantage of again / David J. Lieberman.
p. cm.
Includes bibliographical references.

ISBN 10: 0-978-63130-7
ISBN 13: 978-0-978-63130-7

1. Interpersonal communication. 2. Social
perception. 3. Truthfulness and falsehood.   I. Title.

BF637.C45L515 2006   153.6   QBI06-600339
Library of Congress Control Number: 2006933983
March 2007

Design: Desktop Publishing Ltd. desktoppublishing@shaw.ca

Contents

Section I
The Seven Basic Questions
Learn how to find out, quickly and easily,
what anyone is thinking and feeling in any
situation or circumstance.

Chapter 1:   Is this Person Hiding Anything? | 15
Don't get the wool pulled over your eyes! The next time you
suspect someone is hiding something, use these techniques to
casually find out if anyone—kids, co-workers, employees, or
friends—is keeping something from you.

Chapter 2:   Thumbs Up or Down:
Does He Like It or Not? | 29
When you can't figure out if a person has a favorable or unfavorable impression of someone or something, employ these
strategies to learn what he is really thinking regardless of what
he says.

Chapter 3:   Is She Confident or Just Trying to
Play It Cool? | 43
Want to know if the person sitting across the table from you
really has a full house? Is your top executive serious about quitting if he doesn't get a raise? The next time you're in an interrogation, negotiation, or just playing poker, use these
techniques to find out if your opponent is feeling good about
his chances or simply putting up a good front.

Chapter 4:   How Are Things… Really? | 57

How did your co-worker's meeting go? Is your new neighbor's girlfriend a keeper or on the way out? Is your employee truly happy with his new assignment? These tactics will reveal to you what someone is really feeling regardless of how tight-lipped he is.

Chapter 5:   Gauging Interest Levels: Is He Interested, or Are You Wasting Your Time? | 69

Does your date like you or not? Does your co-worker really want to help you with your project? Is your prospect really interested in your product? Use these techniques to quickly find out.

Chapter 6:   Ally or Saboteur: Whose Side Is She Really On? | 81

Is she for you or out to get you? If you think someone who appears to be cooperating is really sabotaging your efforts, follow this strategy to quickly find out whose side she's really on.

Chapter 7:   Emotional Profile: Learn How Safe, Stable, and Sane a Person Is. | 95

Through casual observance or a two-minute conversation, you can learn the warning signs of emotional instability and the potential for violence. Gain the advantage of knowing what to look for—in anyone—and what questions to ask to protect you and your loved ones.

Section II
Blueprints to the Mind—
Understanding the Decision-making Process

Go beyond reading basic thoughts and feelings: Learn how people think so you can profile anyone, predict behavior, and understand a person better than he understands himself.

Don't fall prey to the five most common mistakes when evaluating a person's level of self-esteem! Learn the differences between a person who likes himself (self-esteem) and a person who is simply full of himself (big ego).

Learn the fool-proof method to quickly and easily determine how much self-esteem another person really has.

Find out how to gauge anyone's general outlook on himself, and on his life, based upon the three major profiles.

Sharpen your skills and see how to apply your new understanding of human nature with real-life examples.

How to Use the Book

Section I of this book shows you how to speed-read other people to quickly determine their basic thoughts, feelings, and emotions. The system works with any person, place, idea, or situation. For example, in just minutes you can determine if someone is interested or not, confident or scared, being honest, or hiding something.

In this section, we focus on seven major questions you may have regarding another's thoughts and intentions by using an array of real-life examples to illustrate how the techniques are easily applied. Each chapter in the book contains a variety of observational and conversational techniques.

In some cases, you will not be able to directly engage the person from whom you need information in conversation. In these situations, you'll use a strategy that employs a variety of signs and signals. At other times, you'll be able to interact with the individual in question, so more sophisticated strategies can be used.

Section II comes into play when there are situations in which you will want greater insight. In this section, you will learn how to build a near-perfect profile of anyone, how to tell what someone is thinking or feeling, and how to predict what he or she will do next.

For instance, by applying the techniques in Section I, you will be able to tell if your date is interested in you. Then, you can later do a complete profile if you want to know how he or she will respond to anything you say or do. When negotiating, you can quickly measure the other party's levels of honesty and confidence.

But if you want to know how he will proceed, how to measure his flexibility, or detect his hot buttons, you can use this psychological strategy to quickly and discreetly build a complete profile.

Using specific, real-world examples, you will learn how to tell whether a juror will be hard or easy to sway, if a guilty suspect will confess or stick to his story, or if a person will be forgiving or unforgiving when he finds out an unpleasant truth.

This book will teach you how to get to the bottom of any situation, keep from being taken advantage of, and get the upper hand with anyone, anytime—often in five minutes or less.

Introduction

Have you ever wished you could peer into someone's mind to find out what he's really thinking? Now you can, using a highly advanced, psychologically based system. As the only one of its type, this program offers a complete, practical, and easy-to-use system that you can use to measure a person's thoughts and feelings quickly, at any time.

To be clear, *You Can Read Anyone* is not a collection of recycled ideas about body language. We are not going to suggest a woman's hairstyle will give you unlimited access to her soul or draw wildly ambiguous generalities about people based on our intuition or gut instincts. This book will not tell you how to reach conclusions based on how someone folds his hands or ties his shoelaces.

The principles herein are not ideas, theories, or tricks that only work sometimes on some people. The book contains specific, proven psychological techniques that can instantly be applied to any person in almost any situation.

Does this mean you will be able to read anyone with perfect precision, every time? No. The system is not 100 percent foolproof. However, you will gain a definitive statistical advantage in every encounter. You'll have the ability to use the most important psychological tools governing human behavior to not only level the playing field but also to create an automatic advantage.

Please understand, this book is not about developing so-called "telepathy" so you can learn how to know exactly what number someone is thinking or whether someone is considering having a tuna-fish sandwich for lunch.

You Can Read Anyone shows, step-by-step, how to tell what anyone is thinking and feeling in real-life situations. For example, you will see exactly how to predict whether another poker player will stay in or fold, whether a salesperson is trustworthy, or whether a first date is going your way or the other way.

When the stakes are high, do more than simply put the odds in your favor. Set up the game so you can't lose.

SECTION I

THE 7 BASIC QUESTIONS

Learn how to find out quickly and easily, what anyone is thinking and feeling in any situation or circumstance.

- Is This Person Hiding Anything?
- Thumbs Up or Down—Does He Like It or Not?
- Is She Confident or Just Trying to Play it Cool?
- How are Things . . . Really?
- Is He Interested, or are You Wasting Your Time?
- Whose Side Is She Really On?
- How Safe, Stable, and Sane Is a Person.

Is This Person Hiding Anything?

CHAPTER 1

"*Honesty may be the best policy, but it's important to remember that apparently, by elimination, dishonesty is the second-best policy.*"

George Carlin

When you have a sneaking suspicion that another person may be up to something underhanded, you are left with three bleak options: confront the person, ignore the situation, or try to gather more information.

If you confront the person, not only does it put him or her on the defensive, but if it turns out you are wrong, there is a good chance you may appear paranoid or jealous and the relationship will suffer.

Ignoring the situation can be difficult and possibly damaging to you.

Finally, trying to gather more facts on your own is time-consuming and can work against you if you get caught snooping around.

Whenever you have a gut feeling that something dishonest is going on—such as your teenage child doing drugs, a stealing employee, or a disloyal friend—use one of the following techniques to find out what a person is really up to or has on his mind.

Technique 1: The Mind Reader

This technique, which I originally introduced in my book *Never Be Lied to Again*, virtually guarantees that you can find out within minutes if someone has something to hide. It works like a Rorschach test, also commonly referred to as an ink-blot test. The Rorschach test consists of abstract, bilaterally symmetrical splotches of inkblots. The theory behind the test is that a person's interpretation of the shapes will reveal his or her unconscious attitudes and thoughts.

With our technique, we use the same theory, but employ it in an entirely new way—*verbally*. You ask a question that does not accuse the other person of anything but does allude to the situation. Then, simply by gauging the response, you'll be able to find out if the person has something to hide.

By doing this, you can bring up a sensitive subject and find out if someone is comfortable or concerned with the topic, all without making a single accusation. Let's look at an example:

SNAP SHOT A sales manager thinks one of his salespeople may be stealing office supplies. Asking outright, "Have you been stealing from the company?" would put the employee on the defensive immediately, making it nearly impossible to get the truth out of her. If she's not guilty, she'll, of course, tell the manager that she hasn't been stealing. If she is guilty, she will probably lie and say she hasn't pilfered any supplies. Instead, the manager might simply say something non-threatening, such as, "Jill, I'm wondering if you could help me with something. It's come to my attention that someone in the sales department has been taking home office supplies for personal use. Do you have any idea how we can put a stop to this?" Now he simply observes her reaction.

If she asks questions and seems interested in the topic of conversation, he can be reasonably sure she is not stealing, but if she becomes very uneasy and seeks to change the subject, then it's likely that she's guilty.

The manager will notice an immediate shift in her demeanor and attitude. (For detailed signs of anxiety and insecurity, please see Chapter 3).

If she is innocent, she's likely to offer her advice and be pleased he sought out her opinion. If guilty, she'll become noticeably uncomfortable and probably will assure him that she would never do anything like stealing. No reason exists for her to bring herself into the picture unless, of course, she is the one who feels guilty.

Another way to apply the technique is to simply wonder aloud how someone could do a particular thing (what you think the other is doing) and gauge the person's response. Let's see how wondering aloud works:

SNAPSHOT   A woman thinks her date is acting slightly odd, and wonders if he is taking some kind of substance—prescribed or otherwise. To find out, she can ponder aloud, "Isn't it interesting that people can use drugs and think that others don't know?" Alternatively, she could say, "I was just reading an article that said 33 percent of adults have tried recreational drugs at one time or another in their lives."

She indirectly raises the subject, observing whether his reaction will indicate if he is hiding his own drug use. Someone who's not engaged in the actions she mentions is likely to join in the conversation willingly, while someone who is involved in the behavior will move to shift the topic of conversation.

This technique can also be applied by actually asking the other person for his advice.

SNAP SHOT A hospital administrator suspects a doctor is drinking on duty. She might say, "Dr. Smith, I'd like to get your advice on something. A colleague of mine at another hospital has a problem with one of her doctors. She feels he may be drinking while on call. Do you have any suggestions on how she can best approach this doctor?"

Again, if he is guilty of the same behavior, drinking on duty, he is likely to become very uncomfortable. If he isn't drinking on duty, then he will be pleased you sought his advice and will offer it willingly and happily.

Technique 2: Paging Dr. Bombay

If you think someone knows someone or something specific, the "Paging Dr. Bombay" technique can be used to help find the truth. The technique works on a psychological principle: a person is drawn equally to what he has no prior knowledge of. Simply, if a person has never heard of Fred, Peter or Marvin, his interest in them will be equal. Conversely, his attention will naturally be drawn to what he is most familiar with. If he knows Marvin but not the other two, he'll pay more attention when Marvin's name is mentioned, in contrast to the other names.

This technique presents the person with evenly available options. If his interest moves unevenly in one direction, it's likely that he has an awareness of certain information that he has not revealed to you. Here's how it works:

SNAP SHOT A personnel manager thinks Jimmy may be planning to leave the company and take a list of clients with him. He suspects Jimmy has already met with "Mr. Black," the owner of a competing company.

Therefore, the manager simply sits Jimmy down and casually puts three folders on the desk labeled "Mr. Green," "Mr. Blue," and "Mr. Black." If Jimmy already has met, or is planning to meet with Mr. Black, his gaze will at first fix longer on Mr. Black's file than on the other files. Then he may try to avert his focus from the file whereby his attention will appear mechanical and uneven.

Another way to apply the technique is by merely talking about the situation and listening for his focus. First, state all the facts as you both know them to be. Then, *switch one of them*. If his attention goes to the switched fact, then you know conclusively that he is aware of the situation itself.

For example, let's say a detective is interviewing a suspect about a robbery. He reads from the report, telling his suspect exactly what happened, but switches a key point about the facts of the crime. If the suspect is guilty, his attention will instinctively go to the key point. What he hears surprises him. He wants to be sure he heard you right, and he will use the "inconsistency" as a reason why he could not have committed the crime. The only way he would know to focus on one "fact" would be if he committed the crime. If he's innocent, then all of the crime's details are unknown to him, so he's incapable of separating them into "true" or "false" categories. Let's see what this dialogue sounds like in action:

DAVID J. LIEBERMAN

SNAP SHOT The detective reads the "facts" to his suspect as he knows them. "The suspect shot the teller, left in a green sedan with California license plates, (then add one piece of false information) crashed into another car, got out, jumped over a fence and got away."

If the suspect is guilty, he will question the incorrect detail: "Crashed into another car? My car doesn't have a scratch on it. It couldn't have been my car!" His "proof" of innocence uses the one false piece of information; by using it, he reveals he knows the whole story.

Technique 3: What Do You Think?

The key to this technique is to not accuse, but inform. Your subject's response will tell you if he's hiding anything. The sequence explores a person's frame of mind when he is presented with new information.

For example, Pauline visits her doctor for a routine physical. When her doctor gets the blood test results back, he calls to inform her she has contracted the herpes virus. Thinking back over her recent sexual partners, she's convinced that Mike or Howie must have given her the disease. Merely asking her two "suspects" if they knowingly gave her herpes would most likely prove futile, as denial by both would be likely. Here is what she does:

SNAP SHOT Pauline calls both guys and casually informs them she just found out she has herpes. The responses she receives lead her straight to the culprit. After hearing the news, the two men respond as follows:

Mike: "Well, don't look at me! I didn't give it to you! I'm clean."

Howie: "You what?! How long have you had it? You might have given it to me! I can't believe this. Are you sure?"

Who is most likely to be the guilty party? If you guessed Mike, you're right. On hearing that Pauline has an incurable, easily transmittable disease, he goes on the defensive, assuming he is being accused of infecting her with herpes. He is unconcerned about his own health because he already knows he is infected. All he wants is to convince Pauline that he's not guilty.

Howie, in contrast, assumes the call is to inform him she might have infected him. Thus, he gets angry because he is concerned about his health.

Simply, a person wrongly accused will be more likely to go on the offensive, while the guilty party usually assumes a defensive posture. Here's another example:

S N A P   S H O T   Let's say you're working in the customer-service department of a computer store. A customer brings a non-working printer back for an exchange, claiming he bought it a few days ago. He has the all-important receipt, and the printer is packed neatly in the original box.

Upon inspecting the contents, you find a necessary, expensive, and easily removable component of the machine missing—a clear indication of why the machine is not functioning properly. Here are two possible responses you might get after informing the customer of your discovery:

Response 1: "I didn't take it out. That's how it was when I bought it."

Response 2: "What? You sold me a printer that has a missing part. I wasted two hours trying to get the thing to work!"

Do you see how effective this is? The person who gives Response 2 has every right to be annoyed, and goes on the offensive. It never crosses his mind that he's being accused of anything.

The person who gives Response 1 knows he never tried to get the printer to work, because he took the part out. It does not occur to him to become angry. He automatically assumes he's being accused of removing the part and becomes defensive when informed the part is missing.

Technique 4: Dodge or Declare

When using this technique, the object is to attach your suspicion to something you know is true about a person but completely unrelated. If he tries to hide or deny the truth about what you know for sure, you have the answer to your suspicion.

However, if he freely acknowledges the existence of your claim but denies the relationship, then your suspicion is likely untrue. Let's take a look:

SNAP SHOT Henry wonders if his date is an alcoholic. He already knows Elaine always chews gum after her meals; a likely unrelated (and certainly benign) activity. Therefore, he would say something such as, "I was reading a study that alcoholics tend to chew gum after meals."

Now, if Elaine is an alcoholic, he will notice she will, in addition to becoming uncomfortable, probably choose to not chew the gum after eating.

You see, she will have no reason to deviate from her usual behavior unless it shows her in an unflattering light. Moreover, she has no reason to doubt the veracity of Henry's research statement.

She is probably thinking, "Yikes, that's just what I do." However, if she is not an alcoholic, she will say to him she always chews gum after meals, so the study cannot be completely true. Of course, she may not chew the gum to avoid her date assuming otherwise even if she does not drink excessively. But the odds are she won't deny herself an enjoyable routine and give up a chance to refute his "study" merely to avoid presenting a wrong appearance.

Technique 5: Fear of Folly

When stakes are high, "Fear of Folly" is a great technique to determine what someone's hiding, regardless of how good an "actor" he may be. To apply the psychology of the technique, you inform your subject he and another person—a confederate working with you—are both "suspects," and you "attach" an unwelcome quality to the person who is guilty.

DAVID J. LIEBERMAN

Then, gauge your subject's behavior. If interaction with the other person causes him concern, it's likely that he's innocent.

SNAP SHOT A police detective puts his suspect into a holding cell and declares, "Okay. We know one of you is guilty, and blood found at the scene tells us the perpetrator has hepatitis C." Now, when the confederate, bleeding from his hand, approaches your suspect, if he's not guilty, he'll move away and become alarmed. He knows the other guy must be responsible.

However, if he's guilty, he has no reason to be concerned about this person having hepatitis. He assumes he has hepatitis because he already knows he's guilty.

You can also use this technique in groups by merely attaching your marker to the suspicion and not the suspect. Subsequently, the suspect will show himself.

SNAP SHOT A manager wanting to find out who went through his desk might say, "Whoever went into the office will be fired. The rest of you will get a promotion for enduring this investigation." Now, he simply observes his suspect's subsequent behavior. If he is excited or inquires about the salary and benefits of the new job, then he's probably innocent. Otherwise, sitting silently demonstrates a strong sign he was behind the "break-in."

Technique 6: How Would You Do It?

This technique works under the premise that a guilty person will do whatever he can to give the impression of innocence. By asking outright how your suspect would do the very thing that you accuse him of, you gain a great insight into his thinking. The psychological assumption is this: when a situation presents only one reasonable way to do something and the person picks an out-of-the-box answer, it is worthy of further investigation.

SNAP SHOT Helen believes her bookkeeper, Mitch, has been skimming money from a petty funds account. Embezzling would be easy for him because there are no real checks-and-balances. While he denies stealing money, she has her suspicions.

Therefore, in a light, carefree moment, she says: "If you were to steal, how would you go about doing it?" If he responds with a convoluted answer like, "Well, thinking off the top of my head, I'd keep a separate set of books and then use invisible ink . . . " he's probably hiding something.

Why? The right answer would be to do it the easy way—by taking money from petty funds. However, since he doesn't want her to know he has thought of petty funds, he comes up with a roundabout way of stealing.

QUICK TAKE A traveler comes to a fork in the road leading to two villages. In one village, the people always tell lies, and in the other village, the people always tell the truth. The traveler needs to conduct business in the village where everyone always tells the truth. A man from one of the villages is standing in the middle of the fork, but there is no indication of which village he resides in. The traveler approaches the man and asks him just one question. From the man's answer, he knows which road to follow. What did the traveler ask?[1]

---

1   *"Which way to your village?"* He goes that way. Remember, he needs to go to the truth-tellers. If the man is telling the truth, he will direct him in the right direction. If the man is telling a lie, he will direct him in the right direction. Either way, he knows which way to go. An alternative solution is to ask, "What would the other person tell me to do?" Then, go the other way.

2

Thumbs Up Or Down: Does He Like It Or Not?

CHAPTER

"There's only one thing worse than a man who doesn't have strong likes and dislikes, and that's a man who has strong likes and dislikes without the courage to voice them."

Tony Randall

Have you ever been in a meeting with someone but found yourself unable to determine what's going through her head? Has someone you know had an unusual experience but won't tell you what she thinks about it? When you explain a new strategy to a co-worker, he barely says a word. What is he thinking?

This chapter will teach you how, in similar situations, to quickly and discreetly discover what a person is really thinking, sometimes without saying a single word.

Technique 1: The Ghost Image

When you write a message down on a note pad and tear off the sheet, have you ever noticed what happens? Usually, the message is still legible on the paper underneath. The indentation of the pen causes the message to remain even after you remove the top sheet. The process is analogous to our technique, because all of our experiences leave an impression on things around us and can create a conditioned response. Let's explain:

Do you remember the lessons learned by Russian scientist Pavlov? In short, the dogs he worked with salivated when he walked into the room. The dogs had learned Pavlov's appearance meant they would be fed soon and therefore associated Pavlov with food, even without the presence of food. The example is referred to as a conditioned reflex, and we have many examples in our own lives.

For instance, maybe the smell of cut grass brings back fond memories of your childhood; or, anytime you meet someone with a certain name you have unpleasant feelings towards them because of a former experience with a person of the same name.

Memories are anchors. An anchor is an association or link between a specific set of feelings or emotional state and some unique stimulus: an image, sound, name, or taste.

By associating the current situation with a neutral stimulus, a person's true feelings attach themselves to the stimulus.

In a classic 1982 study, Gerald Gorn paired one pen color with pleasant music and another pen color with unpleasant music. (The two pen colors, blue and beige, are used in the experiment with similar positions). Gorn split the subjects of the experiment into separate groups and showed them both the blue pen and the beige pen paired with "pleasant" music (in this case, the *Grease* soundtrack), or "unpleasant" music (in this case, classical Indian music).

At the end of the experiment, the subjects were told they could keep one of the pens as a gift. By a 3.5 to 1 ratio, the subjects picked the pen paired with the music they preferred (Gorn, 1982).

Another study, illustrating the same conditioning phenomenon was conducted at the University of Warsaw (Lewicki, 1985). During the study, students were interviewed by a researcher and then asked to state their name and "birth order." Whenever a subject asked what "birth order" means, the interviewer lambasted the student for his ignorance or reacted neutrally by merely answering the question.

The students were further instructed to go into another room and hand a piece of paper to "whichever researcher is not busy." Both researchers in the room were "not busy." However, one researcher physically resembled the interviewer. An astounding *80 percent* of the subjects who had been scoffed at chose the researcher who did not resemble the "birth order" interviewer. Alternatively, about 45 percent of the subjects receiving the neutral response chose the look-alike.

With this technique, we apply the same psychological process by pairing the situation with a neutral stimulus and merely observing his "feelings" toward the stimulus. If he becomes more attracted to it, you know he has a favorable impression of what was previously unknown. Conversely, if he displays an unusual dislike for it, you know unpleasant feelings are transplanted from the original source.

SNAP SHOT You are a mediator working to resolve a dispute between two parties. After extensive negotiations, you are having trouble reading both of them. On the desk are several blue pens. After the meeting, you ask both parties to individually sign several, preferably unrelated documents—eliminating the possibility of individual preference or unnecessary consistency—over the course of a few minutes. The parties give the pen back to you each time. Each time you ask them to sign, you offer a choice between black and blue pens.

Assuming the pens are equally desirable, the party consistently choosing the black pen probably has a negative association with the blue pen and unfavorable feelings about the previous discussion. However, the party overwhelmingly picking the blue pen presumably has positive feelings associated with the pen and favorable impressions toward the meeting. The psychological strategy can be used with a variety of paired associations, giving you a strong statistical edge in fishing out a person's preferences.

SNAP SHOT A person is listening to your presentation. You are both seated in blue chairs. Afterwards, he is taken to a new room with a round table and four chairs: two blue and two gray. If he has a favorable impression of the talk, statistically speaking, he is more likely to choose the blue chair over the gray one.

Anytime the person is "attracted" to the stimulus present during the situation in question, we assume his impression was positive. In contrast, when a person is repelled by a previous neutral stimulus, we assume he has an unfavorable impression.

Before we continue with more techniques, let's look at a couple of highly reliable signs to a person's true thinking:

Signal I: First Impressions
Dr. Paul Ekman, psychologist and leading lie-detection expert, points out a clue to true feelings in the form of micro-facial expressions—emotional responses reflecting a person's true feelings. The expressions flash across a person's face too quickly for most to see, and the person quickly adjusts his expression to give off the desired impression (Ekman,1985). You need not worry about videotaping the scenario.

While you may not be able to detect the initial emotional response, the fact that a new one appears is evidence of a mask for his true feelings. Whatever impression he is exhibiting now, if his expression took a while in coming or changed from something else, then assume it is not genuine. Ekman points out most people are not aware of micro-expressions, since they appear before they can be morphed and probably before the person experiencing the emotion is even aware of the emotion.

Signal 2: The Unconscious Spills

The use of pronouns can reveal a fascinating insight into someone's true thoughts and feelings. "Statement Content Analysis" is a system that examines the use of pronouns such as "I" and "we." For example, it is unusual for victims of abductions, sexual batteries, and other violent crimes to refer to the offender and victim as "we."

Instead, in recounting narratives involving the crime, the victim usually uses the personal pronoun "I" to refer to himself and "he" or "she" to the offender. The use of the personal pronoun "we" involves a psychological closeness not typical in a crime (Adams, 1996).

SNAP SHOT   A friend is telling you about her night out with her boyfriend. Her story is peppered with the word we: "We got to the club at 10 o'clock .. then we had a drink . . . we met some of his friends . . . " Then, the narrative changes to, "He took me home." You can rightly assume there was a dispute of some sort between your friend and her boyfriend, since she moves to a less intimate recounting. For example,

"We drove home; we went home; we left" and so on, would more likely indicate a harmonious ending.

Many applications of this psychology exist. For instance, when a person is confident and believes in what he is saying, he is more likely to use the pronoun "I," "we," or "us." When we feel less strongly, we unconsciously seek to distance ourselves from our remarks and do not attach ownership to our words.

SNAP SHOT If you ask your boss what she thinks of your new idea and she responds by saying "I like it," you have a higher probability of truthfulness. If she says, "It's nice," or "You did a good job," she does not take ownership of her sentence and may not believe in what she is saying.

It is important to remember that all signs must be examined within the context of the situation, and we should avoid a definitive conclusion based upon isolated signals.

QUICK TAKE A key component to graphology (handwriting analysis) looks at the distance between the pronoun "I" and the next word to help determine the author's true feelings. If the distance is greater than the spacing between other words, we assume there is an unconscious attempt, by the writer, to distance himself from the statement. Additionally, if the pronoun is smaller or lighter (less pressure), then there is reason to believe the writer is conflicted or outright does not believe firmly in what he is writing.

Technique 2: All The World Is a Reflection

It is often said that a person looks at the world as a reflection of himself. If he sees the world as a corrupt place, he feels at some level—albeit probably unconsciously—that he is corrupt. If he sees honest working people, that is often how he sees himself. As the saying goes, "It takes one to know one." Out of the blue and with no real evidence, if someone thinks you are up to something, ask yourself, "Why is he so paranoid?"

In psychological terms this is referred to as projection. Projection is why the con artist is the first one to accuse another of cheating. If you are constantly being questioned about your motives or activities, the accusations should set off alarm bells in your mind.

How often do we hear of a jealous boyfriend constantly accusing his girlfriend of cheating on him, only to have her find out he is guilty of everything he has been accusing her of doing? The methodology is applied in the following way:

If you ask someone if he is an honest person, he may simply lie and say "yes." However, if you were to ask if he thinks most people are honest, he's free to give his opinion without concern for your ascribing the quality to him.

A window into his soul, though? Not exactly.

Transparency is obviously a concern—you want to make sure he will not know what you are really asking. Therefore, we use the transitive property to draw out his true feelings without arousing suspicion. In mathematics, the transitive property of equality is illustrated by: if $a = b$ and $b = c$, then $a = c$.

Let's say you want to find out if a person is in a happy marriage. Of course, simply asking outright is not a mind-reading technique, nor can you be assured of accuracy.

Therefore, we use the following system to more specifically pinpoint his feelings without running the risk of transparency or anomaly. Using correlated information—one or two steps removed from the original question—you can penetrate his real attitude without him thinking he is giving away his true feelings.

SNAP SHOT The question is, "Are you happy in your marriage?" The primary correlated statistic is: people who are happy in marriage are grateful for their spouse. The secondary correlated statistic is: a person who is grateful for his spouse tends not to take advantage of her. The question asked is, "Do you think taking advantage of your spouse is simply part of marriage?"

If he responds by saying, "Yes," this is a red flag (though certainly *not* conclusive) that he may not be *thoroughly* happy in marriage, as he is taking advantage of his spouse, feels she takes advantage of him, or both.

Naturally, coming up with the right correlations is essential. There is no hard-and-fast formula—it is not foolproof, but it does bend the odds in your favor. Some correlations are statistically oriented, while others are simply common sense. Let's see another example:

SNAP SHOT A defense attorney wants to find out whether a potential juror is for or against the death penalty. If he cannot ask directly or worries he cannot be sure of a truthful answer if he does ask, he uses a correlated fact: *statistically speaking, a person who is for the death penalty is against gun control.* Now, he simply asks the juror if she is for or against gun control. If he believes the question is still too transparent, he can further correlate it with a question such as, "Do you think gun manufacturers should be held responsible for misuse or abuse of their products?" Accordingly, he assumes that a person who supports gun control is likely to believe gun manufacturers have a greater degree of liability than someone who does not support gun control.

Thus, the technique gives you a greater insight into the person's true thinking and, combined with other techniques in this section, can help you to know what is really going on his head.

QUICK TAKE Our physical selves are highly tuned to that which is unhealthy—false. For instance, one interesting test shows the effects of various substances on the human body. If a person holds his arm in front of his body, he will resist another person pushing his arm down. However, once the person places a small sample of an unhealthy substance, like refined sugar, in his hand, the ability for his arm to maintain the same levels of strength is often significantly diminished.

DAVID J. LIEBERMAN

Technique 3: Language Lessons

Language powerfully impacts how we perceive and, consequently, feel about what we hear. Good salespeople know they should suggest to a customer "Okay the paperwork" instead of "Sign the contract." Beware when a person uses a euphemism, an expression intended by the speaker to be less offensive or disturbing to the listener than the word or phrase it replaces.

For example, the military understands the influence of words on attitude and behavior. People are more comfortable hearing about a military action than a war, even though the terms mean the same thing. We would rather hear about collateral damage than civilian property and lives being accidentally destroyed. Casualties are easier to swallow than deaths, and friendly fire is preferred over hearing we shot at our own forces.

In everyday life, we do the same thing: we may refer to the toilet as the bathroom, the powder room, the men's room, or ladies' room. Indeed, we would rather tell our insurance company of the "fender-bender" than use the word "collision." And of course, letting an employee "go," or telling him he is being laid-off, is often the preferred language over being "fired."

So what is the practical application here? In a subtle way, sometimes even unconsciously, the language a person uses reveals if he is concerned you will not like, accept, or believe the news.

SNAP SHOT After reviewing Theresa's proposal, her supervisor declares, "Your idea is interesting," "thought-provoking," or "nicely written." Without any follow-up, Theresa can assume he did not like the proposal.

Of course, a person's style of communication, among other variables, must be taken into consideration. However, absent any other information and in conjunction with one or two other techniques in this section, you will gain a much greater insight into the situation. Usually, a person will directly say what he means, unless he has a reason to deviate. Let's examine another scenario:

SNAP SHOT Fred's new girlfriend mentions she stopped by to see someone with whom she was "friendly" some time ago. If she had said dated, as was the case, Fred could assume not much is going on. Her decision to use a euphemism means she believes Fred would not take kindly to her whereabouts or she is not revealing the larger picture.

Technique 4: Positive Markers

In the previous chapter, we spoke about using negative markers (remember gum chewing and alcoholism?) to find out if someone's up to something. Here, we use positive markers to detect whether a person has a favorable or unfavorable impression about something.

SNAP SHOT After two meetings with a new law firm, Ryan wants to find out how interested the firm is in him. Therefore, he may say, "I'd be really excited about working for a firm that has a passion for pro-bono work instead of treating it as an obligation." Now, Ryan gauges the response.

If the other person elaborates on the firm's commitment to pro-bono work and puts forth his own personal commitment, there is a good chance the firm is very interested in Ryan. However, if he goes right by the point or offers a light agreement, they are less likely to be interested in him: he may be wasting his time.

To make the technique work, the marker should be something subjective, allowing the person the option of attaching himself to the marker, or ignoring it.

Is She Confident or Just Trying To Play It Cool?

CHAPTER 3

"Self-confidence is the first requisite to great undertakings."

Samuel Johnson (1709 - 1784)

I s the poker player sitting across the table from you confident or scared? Is your date really as sure of himself as he wants you to believe? Is the opposing lawyer as happy with his case as he professes? Use these techniques to find out if your opponent is feeling good about his chances or just putting up a good front.

To better understand confidence, we must first clear up a misnomer. Self-esteem is often confused with confidence, but the two are quite different. The distinction is very important. Confidence is how effective a person feels within a specific area or situation, while self-esteem is defined by how much a person "likes" himself and how worthy he feels of receiving good things in life. Simply, a person can feel good about himself yet not feel positive about his chances under certain circumstances, and vice-versa.

For instance, an attractive woman may feel confident she can find a date in the bar, but finding a date has nothing to do with how she feels about herself overall. Likewise, a man who has high self-esteem may be a lousy chess player, but he "likes" himself. He will exhibit signs of deteriorated confidence when playing with a superior player, yet his self-worth remains unaffected.

A person's confidence in a particular situation is based on a variety of factors: previous performance, experiences, feedback, and comparisons. As well, self-esteem can affect confidence. Studies show the greater someone's self-esteem, the more inclined he is to feel comfortable and confident in a new situation.

However, the opposite is not true. A person placing a great degree of importance on confident feelings (i.e. physical appearance, considering himself to be attractive) may exhibit signs of higher self-esteem to the untrained eye. Nevertheless, a person's feelings of self-worth are affected more by what he does (free-will behavior) and not what he is or what assets are at his disposal. Therefore, what we may perceive as self-esteem is really an inflated ego.

Self-esteem and confidence are distinct psychological forces, and both impact the overall psyche differently. While it's interesting to note the source and impact, the origin does not bear any consideration in terms of evaluation. Whether or not the person is confident is the only thing we need to assess here. Where and how it came about is not necessary to our evaluation. So, let's return to our immediate discussion and see precisely how to gauge someone's level of confidence.

> **QUICK TAKE** When we are anxious or stressed, our ability to focus is often diminished. Have you ever met someone at a party and forgotten his name right after you are introduced? Look at distraction and the inability to pay attention to what is going on as signs of temporary insecurity.

Gauging Confidence Levels

Now, we'll examine what a confident person looks and sounds like, so we can readily determine who is and isn't secure. Depending on the situation, we can rely on one or more signs, signals, and techniques.

The real secret to reading someone's confidence level lies not in observation but in filtering out the signs intended to give the *impression of confidence*. We will cover readily known signs of confidence: smiling, eye contact, and so on. But because signs of confidence are easy to fake, we'll turn our discussion to more complex factors that are easy to observe and nearly impossible to manufacture.

Sign 1: The Physical

In instances of extreme fear, when a person is quite uncomfortable, you will notice one of two distinct behaviors: either his eyes will dart around and he will become easily distracted, because he is on emotional high-alert, or he may freeze and do the exact opposite. The familiar "deer-in-the-headlights" reaction is a prime example. Let's look at some other involuntary responses a person has little or no control over:

The Fight-or-Flight Syndrome: A person's face may become flushed, or turn white, with extreme fear. Look for signs of rapid breathing and increased perspiration. Additionally, take note if he is trying to control his breathing to calm himself. Efforts to remain calm will appear as deep, audible inhaling and exhaling.

Trembling or shaking in voice or body: Hidden hands may tremble. If he's hiding his hands, it might be an attempt to hide uncontrollable shaking. His voice may crack and seem inconsistent.

QUICK TAKE   When we are nervous, we take things more
literally. When we lack confidence in a situ-
ation, our mind tries to get its bearings, and we often cannot
see beyond face value. For instance, we will often have trouble processing sarcasm, because it requires a non-logical perspective, and this shift in thinking takes time.

Difficulty swallowing: Swallowing becomes difficult, so
look for a hard swallow. Television or movie actors, who wish
to express fear or sadness, often use this behavior—hence the
expression "all choked up." Throat-clearing also is a sign of
nervousness. Anxiety causes mucus to form in the throat. A
public speaker who is nervous often clears his throat before
speaking.

Vocal changes: Vocal chords, like all muscles, tighten when
a person is stressed, producing a higher sound, octave, or
pitch.

The "Blinker": When people are nervous, their blink rate
increases. In a *Newsweek* article published October 21, 1996,
Boston College Neuropsychology Professor Joe Tecce made
this point regarding the presidential debates of Bob Dole and
Bill Clinton during the primary election: The normal blink rate
for someone on television is 31-50 blinks per minute.

Bob Dole averaged 147 blinks per minute and 3 blinks per
second. His highest rate of 163 blinks occurred when asked if
the country was better off now than it was four years ago.
Clinton averaged 99 blinks per minute and peaked at 117,
when he was questioned about the increase of teen drug use.
Professor Tecce pointed out that in the five elections prior to
2000, the candidate with the higher blink rate during the
debates lost the election.

Sign 2: Determining Focus

Imagine an athlete, musician, or artist who is in "the zone" and flawless in his performance. He is not focused on himself, his looks, or his performance. A basketball player, for instance, shoots the ball with the intention of making a basket. All potential distractions are drowned out. He merely has the intention and he carries it out without attention to himself. He is not *self-aware* or self-conscious. If he becomes self-conscious, he is hyper-aware—distracted from what he's doing—and his attention and focus are divided between himself, his surroundings, and others.

A confident person is able to focus on the objective, and the "I" disappears. A nervous person has an ego consuming his thoughts because of fear, worry, and anxiety, and he can't help but focus on himself. He's literally self-aware of everything he says and does. What were once unconscious actions, such as where his hands are or how he is sitting, become part of a heightened state of awareness. Thus, his actions appear more awkward.

Whether in a meeting, on a date, or in an interrogation, when reaching for an object a person feeling in control of the situation may do so without paying attention to his hand or the object. The insecure person does not feel able to do this because he is unsure of himself; his eyes will likely follow his own movements.

Let's further examine the psychological mechanics involved. There are four stages to someone's actions: *unconscious incompetence* is when a person is unaware that he is not performing correctly; *conscious incompetence* is awareness that he has not acquired the skill set necessary to be as effective and successful as he would like to be; *conscious competence* is when a

DAVID J. LIEBERMAN

person is aware of what he needs to do, but awareness is needed in order to be effective; *unconscious competence* is when a person can perform correctly and as necessary without his full, or even partial, attention.

An analogy of someone who learns to drive a stick shift effectively illustrates the four levels. What is at first completely foreign eventually moves to a skill level at which the driver shifts gears without consciously focusing on what he is doing.

The second, third, and fourth levels give us insight into a person's competency and confidence levels. (The first level is irrelevant, as the person is not even aware of what he is doing, let alone confident at it).

SNAP SHOT During a casual conversation with a co-worker, you notice she reaches for a can of soda well within her grasp. She watches her hand extend to the drink. Then, she watches her hand as it moves up to her lips. Your co-worker is nervous and unsure of herself and does not "trust" her ability to do what she has done hundreds of thousands of times before—take a drink—without paying attention. What is usually a matter of unconscious competence moves down to conscious competence—a heightened level of awareness.

If you know what to look for, confidence (or the lack thereof) is easy to spot. Simply observe whether or not the person is focused on himself and what he is doing. Let's consider another example:

SNAP SHOT A single man walks into a bar, hoping to meet a woman. If he considers himself to be attractive and a good catch, his focus will be on what the women in the bar look like. If he considers himself to be unattractive, he will be more concerned with how *he appears* to them. In other words, his focus shifts depending upon his level of confidence. A lack of confidence forces one to become self-conscious or self-aware. So not only will his demeanor be stiff and mechanical, but his objective is geared towards the impression he is making on others.

We know this to be true in our own lives. For example, when a person has confidence in his words, he is more concerned that you understand him and less interested in how he appears to you. When you're interested in making a point, you want to make sure the other person understands you, but when you're less confident, your focus is internal—on how you sound and appear. You are conscious of your every word and movement.

DAVID J. LIEBERMAN

Advanced Signs & Signals:
Perception-management

When a person is nervous but tries to appear otherwise, this leads to what is called perception-management—a person's attempt to present a certain image in order to convey the "right" effect. We discussed what to look for to tell if a person is confident or insecure. Now, we are looking for something else. We can look for signs of someone trying to *appear* confident. We know a person pretending to be confident is not. Even if he tries to fool you by not giving himself away with the previous signals, you will catch him here, as you learn what a "bluffing" person looks and sounds like.

Sign 1: Overcompensation

A person engaging in perception-management generally overcompensates. If you look for it, it is glaringly obvious. Remember, the confident person is not interested in how he is coming across. He is unconcerned with his image, unlike his perception-management counterpart, who is consumed by others' impressions of him.

SNAP SHOT   A card player bets heavily and raises the pot. Does he have the cards or simply guts? When bluffing in a poker hand, he wants to show he is not timid. He might put in his money quickly. But, if he does have a good hand, what might he do? He will deliberate a bit, putting it in slowly, showing he is not really sure about his hand. Mike Caro, one of the foremost authorities on poker strategy, illuminates numerous instances in his book *Poker Tells* (2003), which revolves around this single aspect of human nature: a bluffing person will give the impression he has a strong hand, while the person with a strong hand will give the impression that his hand is weak.

When people pretend to be confident, in a poker hand or in the real world, they manipulate how confident they appear by trying to create the opposite impression of how they truly feel. Again, while bluffing and trying to appear confident, a player bets quickly. (And when he has a good hand, he will actually wait a moment or two, pretending he's thinking about what to do).

The principle applies in almost every situation. If he reacts too quickly and assuredly, he is trying to show confidence, when in many cases, he really isn't confident. In contrast, a confident person does not need to tell people he is confident. Someone pretending to be sure of himself, or anything else, will make gestures consistent with the attitude, often going a little overboard.

SNAP SHOT Law enforcement professionals know that a person who is lying (and so lacking confidence) will often show deliberative, pensive displays, such as stroking or tapping his chin. He will act as though he is giving serious thought to even the simplest of questions—in an attempt to appear as if he is trying very hard to be helpful.

Another indication of overcompensating with perception-management is when the person unnecessarily tries to regain the psychological advantage.

SNAP SHOT A man drops his date off at her apartment and she declares, "It's late, I think I'm going to go to bed." If he likes her and is insecure, he thinks this is a ruse to get rid of him. He might respond with something such as, "I'm tired too. I wasn't going to stay anyway." He is likely trying not to appear disappointed. However, if he merely says, "Okay, you must be tired," or something to that effect, he is not trying to manage his perception by offering an explanation as to why he doesn't mind.

QUICK TAKE Sometimes, people put up a strong front, knowing they will crumble if they ever have to defend their position. It has been said, the easiest people to sell are those who have a sign saying, "No salesman or solicitors." The reasoning is this: these people know, deep down, if a salesman did get to them, they would buy whatever he had to sell.

Sign 2: Superfluous Gestures

Any superfluous gesture in a serious situation is a sign that someone is trying to act calm and confident. For instance, law enforcement professionals know that a subject may yawn as if to show he is relaxed, calm, or even bored. If the person is sitting, he may slouch or stretch his arms, covering more territory as if to demonstrate comfort. Or, the subject may be busy picking off lint, trying to show he is preoccupied with something trivial and clearly not worried. The only problem is that someone who is wrongly accused will be quite indignant, and not paying attention to such inconsequential activities, nor engaged in promoting the "right" image.

SNAP SHOT A detective is meeting with the parents of a young girl who appears to have been kidnapped. The husband tells the detective the girl may already be dead. Shortly thereafter, he is handed a cup of coffee. If he responds with something such as, "Thank you so much, I need this after a day like today," he is engaging in perception-management and trying to convey he is polite, considerate, and well-mannered... and something is likely very wrong with his story.

Another example of superfluous behavior is trying to look the part. When a person alters his appearance to come across one way and there is no reason for it, he does not really feel what he is portraying.

SNAP SHOT A salesperson of high-end homes meets a potential buyer on a Sunday morning. When the sales agent meets her client, he is dressed in a suit and tie, on his cell phone, and in the middle of an "important" call. He has no money.

QUICK TAKE   The father of motivational research, Ernest Dichter, says in his book, *The Handbook of Consumer Motivations* (1964), " We attempt to escape fear-producing stimuli. By producing fear, we can alter people's behavior. When caught in fear, we regress step by step to ever more infantile and animalistic drives." The more scared a person becomes, the more likely you will see signs of regression, much like the way a person will go for the ice cream or other comfort foods when feeling uneasy, a person's behavior will drift in a regressive direction. Therefore, look for physical manifestations—anything from oral fixation, such as chewing on a pen, to egocentric influences like increased anger, jealousy, resentment, envy, and so on.

Technique 1: Squeezing Signs

When we lack confidence and threat levels increase, signs of insecurity become more visible. Studies conclude that when we are around people we think are better-looking than we are, we tend to feel less confident about our appearance and ourselves. The concept is true, even if we did not feel insecure in the first place.

You see, by introducing a potential threat, we can more easily gauge how comfortable a person really is with himself and the situation. Look for a shift in mood—if he becomes angry, rude, inconsiderate, or exhibits general signs of anxiety or nervousness, then he wants out of the situation.

SNAP SHOT A detective is interviewing a suspect, and the suspect seems confident. Either he is innocent or he is guilty but knows he has got an airtight alibi. When the detective informs the suspect a witness is coming down to the station to see if he fits the description, the suspect may appear relieved if he is confident in his chances, or irritated and agitated if he is not.

QUICK TAKE A person trying to bluff in poker will err on the side of caution by acting kindly towards you. He does not want to risk getting you mad, fearing it may provoke you into calling his bet. Therefore, if you do something that normally annoys him and he remains seemingly unbothered, or uncharacteristically quiet, you can be fairly sure he is not so confident about his chances.

To apply the psychology in any situation, simply reduce his odds of success, and see if he looks squeezed or unbothered.

How Are Things... Really?

CHAPTER 4

"*Don't think you are going to conceal thoughts by concealing evidence that they ever existed.*"
Dwight D. Eisenhower (1890 - 1969)

How did your co-worker's meeting go? Is your new neighbor's girlfriend a keeper or on the way out? Is your employee truly happy with his new assignment? These tactics will reveal to you what someone is really feeling regardless of how tight-lipped he is.

Sign 1: The Power of Perspective

Have you ever experienced the incredible "on-a-roll phenomenon," when absolutely nothing gets in your way? You are unstoppable and succeed every time you try? Then there are times when nothing goes right. Everything you touch seems to go wrong and you're afraid to even get out of bed.

What causes us to get carried along on such a streak? Fascinating research shows it is caused by the way in which our transitional self-concept has been shaped around unfolding events. We see ourselves as that kind of person—hence, we perform in a consistent manner. Even events seemingly beyond a person's complete control can be subject to this law.

Let's take a look at one area and its impact on our self-concept. Studies show when someone is presented with a small request and subsequently honors it, he is infinitely more likely to agree to a larger request—the thing we wanted him to do in the first place. However, if he is not first presented with a smaller request and subsequently does not complete the smaller request, he has no unconscious motivation for consistency.

When we take small steps in one direction, we strive to maintain a sense of consistency by then agreeing to larger requests. Simply, people agreeing to the smaller request have reshaped their self-concept to include the definition: they are serious about driver safety. Therefore, agreeing to the larger request is doing something for a cause they already firmly "believed" in supporting. The effect of this phenomenon extends to many areas of our lives.

If you ask a room full of salespeople whether they have had a similar experience, all hands will go up. For example, you are calling a list of leads and your successes come in streaks. Similarly, you find when things are not going well, they are really not going well. Our world, and how we interact with it, is largely determined by our own perceptions and our perceptions are anchored in our self-concept—the way we see ourselves.

A person's self-concept is generally fixed, but it stretches over a lot of territory and is altered depending upon recent events. Therefore, you can often predict what has happened by taking notice of what is happening.

3 Types: (a) Personal Specific (b) Personal Non-Specific, (c) Generic

(a) Personal Specific:

Research regarding memory and behavior concludes that people base self-concepts on availability or how easily they can bring information to mind. For instance, if you are asked to think of several times when you acted confidently and you are able to recall the events with relative ease, overall, you think of yourself as confident. Conversely, if you cannot come up with an example, you can conclude that you are more cautious and hesitant by nature.

Thus, your subsequent behavior is likely consistent with a cautious and hesitant image, and you are more reserved in your actions. Occasionally, something happens in your life—either to you or caused by you—to make you temporarily reshape the way you see yourself and your world.

> **SNAP SHOT** A salesperson has lost three big accounts in the past few days. The next time he walks into a client's office, he'll be less sure than usual and more hyper-focused. Depending upon interest level and how badly he needs to make the sale, he'll become more anxious and over-analyze the situation to make sure he is "on top of it" and is not missing anything helpful or hurtful. Of course, the exception is a person who has lost several key accounts but can brush

DAVID J. LIEBERMAN

himself off, recite a few affirmations, and meet his next client with renewed vigor and passion. However, this goes against the grain of human nature and is less likely to happen.

SNAP SHOT A poker player has lost two big hands in the past ten minutes. His self-concept is temporarily molded as very unlucky, or one not playing very well. His decision to bluff will be skewed and—all things being equal—he will not do so. Aggressive play will only happen with a strong hand. The general rule: he becomes more "gun shy" and is statistically less likely to take chances.

If you have ever known someone who has had a traffic accident, his subsequent driving changes. For example, if he tried to move into the left lane and did not see the oncoming car that subsequently hit him, he might become more thorough, or even over-thorough, when shifting lanes in the same way again. Or perhaps someone who has been recently rear-ended might glance up at the rear-view mirror more often, out of an exaggerated fear of a repeat scenario.

(b) Personal Non-Specific

Someone's transitory self-concept is also shaped by generic situations. Even something seemingly innocuous, like someone paying you a compliment, can put you in the "I'm-on-top-of-the-world" mode. When things are "going our way," we feel better, more confident and optimistic in other, unrelated situations.

SNAP SHOT Bernard has had his teeth whitened and everyone tells him he looks ten years younger. Therefore, he will be more inclined to take on a new project or get behind an idea that he may have previously resisted.

A person with a renewed sense of confidence likely encountered or was recently thinking about a situation whereby he felt a sense of empowerment, respect, or control.

(c) Generic

Even reading the newspaper can change how we see our world and ourselves. For instance, after hearing about a major plane crash, people tend to overestimate personal vulnerability to the risk of flying. The reason is this: the crash is most available in memory. The odds have not changed, yet our perceptions have changed. Subsequently, our thoughts, attitude, and behavior follow. We literally become more afraid, even though statistically and realistically speaking, nothing has changed.

SNAP SHOT A life insurance salesman calls on a potential customer, Mr. Jones, whose co-worker, a forty-one-year-old man, died of a heart attack two days ago. Mr. Jones' thinking gets warped and his interest level increases. He believes life insurance may be more important than previously suspected.

Whenever you want to gain a glimpse into someone's past, notice how he handles himself in the present. By looking carefully at his actions, you can pick up if his outlook is at all skewed; in which case you can surmise that something recently happened to alter how he currently perceives his reality.

Technique 2: "How Is He Feeling?"

Human beings continually seek purpose and cause in events either unrelated or beyond understanding. Ask the person to observe an unusual yet ambiguous event or happening. If he seems to indicate it is a sign of good fortune, he is feeling optimistic. However, if he says the event is an indication of something negative, he is feeling pessimistic.

SNAP SHOT John walks out of a meeting about a new secret program for which he is trying to garner support. He cannot divulge any of the meeting's details and is putting on his best poker face to avoid giving away any indication that the company will be supporting his plan. If you want to find out, you merely say something such as, "Did you know the office clock stopped at exactly 7:11 and then began running again?" If he responds with something like, "Nothing ever works right around here," you can surmise he is not feeling good about his chances. However, if he responds with a statement such as, "Maybe we should go to Atlantic City and play blackjack," you can assume he is feeling more optimistic about his recent meeting. Regardless of what a person chooses to reveal concerning his feelings, no matter how neutral he tries to be, he often can't avoid the unconscious leaks that spill into the current situation.

Technique 3: Contradictions

Individual gestures need to be looked at separately and in conjunction with what is being said. Besides obvious inconsistencies—such as shaking of the head from side to side while saying yes—subtler but equally revealing signs of someone's true feelings exist.

Whenever you are faced with dual messages, here is the rule of thumb: trust emotional displays over the spoken word. Any time a physical gesture, facial expression, or words are incongruent, you can be fairly sure that what this person says is different from what he believes.

> **SNAP SHOT** A man is frowning or has his fists clenched while professing his love for his girlfriend. He is not feeling very loving toward her. Or your car mechanic, with a faint smile, tells you he is sorry, but the part he ordered came in wrong. Assume he is not sorry, the part is not wrong, or both.

We often witness types of dual messages but quickly dismiss them as our brain seeks to organize information in an easily digestible way. But if we pay attention, we can halt the natural process of information selection and see more clearly what's really going on. Beware of the following signs that the message intended for you is not the real one:

- The timing is off between gestures and words.
- The head moves in a mechanical fashion.
- Gestures do not match the verbal message.
- Emotional gestures' timing/duration seem "off."

Technique 3: A Clean Slate

Generally speaking, the more optimistic a person is about her future, the more forgiving she is of the past. The principle is most evident in situations when the past is directly associated with the future. The psychological link offers us a fascinating window of opportunity to gauge a person's true feelings and thoughts about a current situation by contrasting her feelings to the linked past.

SNAP SHOT Hillary's former business partner, Gary, is pitching to the same potential client as her firm. After Gary's meeting, Hillary simply says something such as, "I'm sorry that things ended the way they did." If Gary is feeling good about his future with this account, he will respond more kindly to Hillary. However, if he thinks his future concerning this account is not positive, his response will reflect his true feelings.

When things are going well for us, we are more forgiving of the negative experiences that got us here in the first place. However, when we feel thwarted or frustrated by what we are doing, we tend to be more hostile toward the people and circumstances causing us to be in "this mess."

SNAP SHOT Gwen wants to know if things are serious with her former fiancée and his new girlfriend, Pam. Of course, she can simply ask, but there is little surety she will get a truthful answer. Therefore, she may say, "I want you to know I valued the time we were together." Now she simply gauges his response. If he is sarcastic and rude, he is probably not feeling too good about his current flame. However, if things are going well with Pam, he will likely respond with something gentler and kinder. Of course, knowing his personality is helpful in setting a baseline. If he usually leans toward being overly sarcastic or overly nice, you need to know before you offer your declaration.

QUICK TAKE Mood is rarely indicative of a person's present situation; it is more often a function of the future and sometimes the past. When in a good mood, a person likely anticipates something pleasurable. One can be on vacation and miserable if he is thinking about going back to work the next day. Conversely, one can be at work thinking about his upcoming vacation in Hawaii and he will be in a terrific mood. Of course, a person can be in a bad mood because of something that happened recently. However, statistically speaking, mood is a function of the future, and if you can rule out a recent past annoyance, you have greater certainty he is thinking of a future event.

Technique 5: Eye-Accessing Cues

Neurolinguistic programming, an offshoot of Miltonian hypnosis, can give you interesting insight into a person's thinking—specifically how thoughts relate to eye movement. For instance, have you ever noticed a daydreaming person stares off into space, usually with his head cocked slightly to the right and eyes to the upper left (for right-handed people)? The following is the general schemata:

When a person looks up, he is accessing or recalling visual information. If a right-handed person looks up and to his left, it indicates he is visually remembering a past event. (For a left-handed person, the opposite is true). We find if a person is looking up and to his left, (your right) he is constructing a visual image.

Generally, most right-handed people move their eyes up for visual, across for auditory, down for language and feelings, right for constructed data, and left for memories.

SNAP SHOT The first thing you want to do is determine if your target fits into the general right or left-handed category. You can do this by simply asking him the color of his first car. Once you have his representation, you are able to detect his real thinking. For instance, you ask your employee why she came in late, and she responds by saying, "There was such a bad car accident right in front of me." Then you might ask something such as, "What color was the car?" If she goes into construct mode, instead of recall mode, you know she's hiding the truth.

5
CHAPTER

Gauging Interest Levels: Is He Interested, or Are You Wasting Your Time?

"Half the time men think they are talking business, they are wasting time."
Edgar Watson Howe (1853 - 1937)

Now, let's find out if your date likes you or not, if your co-worker is really interested in helping you with your project, or if your prospect is interested in your product.

Our ability to gauge whether a person is interested is not difficult, if we can see clearly. The problem is, the more we want something to work out—a date or a sale, for example—the less accurate our ability to objectively discern another person's interest.

When our perspective narrows, we become more neurotic. For example, when pursuing something of perceived importance, such as a project or relationship, we may analyze everything and give it an inflated sense of importance. Our interest has the capacity to consume us, becoming our whole world. Therefore, the best thing we can do is look, as objectively as possible, at the situation and ask, *"If this was happening to a friend of mine, what advice would I give her?"*

A person interested in someone or something shows it, even though he may do or say something to keep his true feelings hidden. This section will cover two techniques, two basic signs of interest and an advanced, nearly foolproof process to quickly gauge anyone's level of interest in anything.

Technique 1: Self-interest

Remember this general rule of thumb: people act in their own best interest. What is the great insight here? Whenever you are questioning a person's desire for something, *consider what he does*, not necessarily what he says.

SNAP SHOT A person saying he is too busy to pursue something of interest is not truthful. And we would see this more often if we were not clouded by our own desire for his interest to be genuine.

Ask this person to invest something, anything—time, money, energy—and see if you get excuses or compliance. The more willing a person is to invest of himself, the more interested he is (assuming you filter out perception-management). Life is a matter of priorities; we all have them, and we make time for what really matters to us. When a person says that he has no time, he often means that it is not worth his time.

Sign 1: The Eyes Have It

Pupil dilation can be a very effective way to gauge someone's interest. When a person is interested or aroused, the pupils dilate, letting in more light, allowing him to "see clearly" and garner more information. When someone is less receptive, the pupils constrict. It is too easy to dismiss the idea as impractical, but please know, if you pay attention you can observe the changes with the naked eye. Researchers Lubow & Fein, (1996) have found that by measuring pupil size in response to photographs of crime scenes, they have been able to detect people with guilty knowledge 70 percent of the time and were able to eliminate people without such knowledge *100 percent of the time.*

In fact, some market research firms install hidden cameras to measure pupil dilation to determine shoppers' responses as they look at different products and packaging. "Pupilometrics" is the name given to the method of advertising research in which a study is conducted of the relationship between a viewer's pupil dilation and the interest factor of visual stimuli.

Additionally, when a person is very interested, look for the eyes to be open wide and, perhaps, for the mouth to be open. Like a child who is surprised with a new toy, his eyes widen and his mouth opens—to take it all in.

S N A P S H O T An art exhibitor shows several pieces to an appraiser, and this is what he observes: the gaze of the appraiser lasts longer on one piece than on the others. Additionally, magnifications of the security camera tapes show his eyes widen and noticeable pupil dilation. The appraiser, regardless of what he says, has a greater interest in this piece than he does the others.

Sign 2: The Eyes Have It, Again!

With heightened interest, a person may be trying to look disinterested, but will keep his attention on the object of his interest. He seeks immediate feedback. Understand, he may not like and may even be fearful of his situation, but we can say he has an elevated level of interest in the outcome.

For instance, a person with a phobia of snakes may become panicked in the presence of the reptile, but her attention will not leave the snake. A person being attacked with a knife will focus on the knife because he wants to know exactly where the knife is at all times.

Yet, understandably, if a grown man is met by a five-year-old wielding a toy knife, his level of attention will not be the same. Only a heightened level of interest will cause a person to focus on an object, as he seeks immediate feedback.

SNAP SHOT A poker player places larger bets than are customary for him and then waits for his opponent to see, raise, or fold. If the player is bluffing, confidence is down, and his interest in what the other player will do is enhanced. We will notice in a novice player that his eyes will continue to glance at his cards or become transfixed, depending on his skill level, on his opponent's hands. He seeks immediate feedback and his opponent's hands will reveal to him what he will do next—go to his chips or fold his cards. If he's not bluffing and less likely to lose, he may glance easily around the room at his opponents' faces and at others. (The more experienced will engage perception-management, though still give themselves away by pretending to be unconcerned).

> **QUICK TAKE** The next time you find yourself in a restaurant, park, or anyplace public or private, and you want to know if someone is interested in you or watching you, look up at the ceiling and transfix on a single point. Then quickly turn around and see where he is looking. If he has been watching you, he will be looking at the same thing you were.

Technique 2: Curiosity Reveals the Cat

"Curiosity Reveals the Cat" is a great technique that works in most situations. The basic premise is this: a person interested in something or someone wants more information than someone not so interested. With the technique, we create a sense of curiosity, and if the person seeks to investigate further, we can say he's at least mildly interested. If he's not curious, then he is uninterested. The secret is to filter out idle curiosity, whereby the person has to do something in order to satisfy his interests. You can apply the psychology of the technique in a myriad of ways.

> **SNAP SHOT** Let's say you want to find out if your old company is still interested in having you come back. You can send your contact a blank e-mail. If she is interested in you, she is curious about what you meant to write (or the file you "forgot" to attach) and will e-mail you back. If not, she will likely ignore the e-mail.

You can also use the technique to see how motivated someone is to do something. You need to create an incentive for him to move; the more energy he invests, the greater his interest is assumed to be.

SNAP SHOT In a small company, Denise wants to find out if a co-worker is interested in moving to another department. She does not think she will get a straight answer by asking him outright. She will say something like, "Tom, I hear accounting has an opening." Of course, he may inquire further about salary, hours, and so on, merely because he is idly curious. Therefore, she ups the ante so that Tom has to invest himself in order to get more information. If he is interested, he will. Denise continues with something such as, "I hear they want someone who's not a clock-watcher and stays late to get the job done." Now, she simply notes whether he leaves as usual or stays on a bit longer.

Technique 3: Shifting Reality

A person's confidence is inversely proportional to his interest level. For instance, a woman who considers herself to be attractive has high confidence in her appearance. If she finds herself in the presence of a man she wants desperately to impress, she will become less confident and secure about herself. Another example is a man who has been out of work for several years. Should he finally land a job interview, his confidence level will be lower than if he was already working and looking to change jobs.

The more interested we are in something or someone, the more consumed and concerned we will be with our ability to obtain the object of our interest. *Our perspective narrows*, and we become hyper-focused. *We observe interest through the lens of confidence and vice-versa.* For example, someone with several job offers is likely to see and evaluate each offer with great objective diligence.

However, when a person has been unemployed for two years, has a stack of bills on his kitchen table, and finally lands a job interview, his perspective is different. He will repeatedly go over the interview, thinking about it nonstop, obsessing over every minute detail, all the while fearing he won't get the job. Such a person is obsessed only because his options are so limited.

When you have the ability to engage the person in conversation, the technique allows you to get a specific reading on the person's degree of interest. Below is a quick outline of each step. We will explore each one in more detail and cover a few examples to show how it all works together.

Step 1: Initial Observation: You want to gauge how interested he appears to be before you say or do anything.

Step 2: Reality Shift: You introduce information, making him believe his chances of getting what he wants are lessened.

Step 3: Observing Response: You simply observe his behavior. If he becomes annoyed or frustrated, he is clearly interested. However, if he does not seem bothered that his chances have dwindled, you may assume he is not so interested.

Step 4: Non-Restrictive: In order to avoid getting a false reading because he may believe he never had a chance and will show no sign of annoyance, you go the "other way" and introduce a reason why he can get what he wants. Now, if he becomes excited, you know he is interested but doesn't believe he can easily succeed in getting what he desires. Let's see what these steps look like in greater depth:

Step 1: Initial Observation

If the person appears to be confident in initial observation, we can conclude (a) he is interested in a favorable outcome and feels good about his chances, or (b) he is not interested. Simply, if he's not interested in something, he may appear confident merely because he doesn't care, not because he is sure of success. And of course, if at first review he appears to be lacking confidence, we conclude interest is high.

Step 2: Reality Shift

Through a "Reality Shift," we reduce a person's perceived chances of being successful and can then gauge his level of interest. Remember, the greater someone's perspective, the more clearly he sees reality; the opposite is also true. By artificially narrowing someone's perspective, the less clearly he sees, forcing him to run toward what he wants.

If you want to know if a person is interested in someone or something, you narrow the possibility of his obtaining it. If his confidence level falls, his level of interest is determined to be high. If his confidence level maintains itself, his interest level is low, thus taking all of the guesswork out of evaluations.

Step 3: Observing Response

Once you engage the "Reality Shift," you merely look for signs of diminished confidence and a shift in mood. A person wanting something but fearing he cannot obtain it will move into a state of constricted consciousness. At the expense of clarifying the obvious, below are signs of both low confidence and poor mood.

- Signs of falling confidence are: inability to pay attention, nervousness, or uncomfortable shifting and posturing (please see previous chapter for more in-depth signs and signals).

- Signs of a diminished mood are: angry, rude, easily frustrated, annoyed, in taking-mode, inconsiderate, or lacking compassion.

Step 4: Non-Restrictive

In what situation might there be great interest yet the person shows no signs of concern even when his chances appear to be dwindling? The answer is, *when the person believes he never had a chance.*

The person, believing he has no likelihood of success, is not confident despite appearances. He is not in the game; we have to put him in the game.

For example, a high school student with a C average who scored a 600 on his SATs is not going to bite his nails over his application to Harvard. Again, if the person feels he has no chance, he will not exhibit signs of nervousness or anxiety over having his odds reduced. To avoid getting a false positive, we want to bring possibility into his realm of reality. If you think he's so cool because he's out of the money, put him in the money and see if it makes a difference.

Now let's put the steps together to see how this technique works in a real-world scenario.

SNAP SHOT A sales agent wants to gauge his client's thoughts. He seems interested, but everyone always does, and the agent wants to know for sure. The salesperson first needs to shift perspective and see if the interest level rises or falls. He will say something like, "Mr. Smith, you should know the finance terms are more restrictive than with most investments." Now he gauges Mr. Smith's response. If he does not seem to care, he clearly has no confidence in his ability to pay back the loan. But if he gets annoyed, there exists both interest and confidence in his ability to pay what he previously assumed was required. Now, it is time for the final shift. If the agent does not perceive much of a change in demeanor, then if could be because the client is willing to accept any terms or he has zero confidence in his ability to make this deal.

The agent informs his customer that he can possibly get him this house with zero down. If the customer begins to ask more questions or becomes giddy, excited, and more animated, the agent knows the house has now become a greater reality for the client. Confidence in his ability to successfully obtain what he wants was initially diminished, based upon the original terms. This confirms high interest and low confidence.

6 Ally or Saboteur: Whose Side Is She Really On?

"It is easier to forgive an enemy than to forgive a friend."
William Blake (1757 - 1827)

I s she for you or out to get you? If you think someone may be sabotaging your efforts when she appears to be cooperating, use the following techniques to find out quickly whose side she's on.

Technique 1: What Can I Do to Help?

The technique works on a simple and known premise: a cooperating person is willing to do what makes sense in order to help. But the saboteur only wants to give the *impression* he is cooperating because he doesn't really want to help you. He is aware that any appearance of cooperation will be viewed more favorably than if he were to overtly refuse to help. The objective becomes to discern if your "suspect" is giving the impression of cooperation or is actually being cooperative.

To accomplish your goal, make his cooperation something he believes is not inherently observable—he is free to act in his own best interest. Meaning, if he is a saboteur, he will try to throw off the test.

Let's say a police detective has a suspect in custody. The interviewer informs the suspect he will shortly be given a test to determine if he is being truthful. In order for the test to work, he must try to remain as relaxed as possible. Otherwise, the test will not work.

Here is the psychology behind the process. The suspect believes the accuracy of the test is contingent upon his level of cooperation. Therefore, if he does whatever he can to cooperate—which in this case is limited specifically to remaining calm—he is innocent. However, if he tries to undermine the effectiveness of the test, you know he does not want to cooperate. Here's what the dialogue might sound like:

SNAP SHOT The interviewer sits the suspect down and says, "Okay John, I think we can clear this up quickly. I'm going to give you a new kind of test that takes only a few minutes. In order for the test to work, it is important you remain as calm and relaxed as possible. Otherwise, it won't work. If you can take some good deep breaths and not move around in the next few minutes, we'll be able to get an accurate reading when we bring in the test. If you fidget or move around, the test won't work and can't be used at all."

Then the interviewer is called away suddenly and leaves the room, while the suspect is observed through the one-way. This "sudden opportunity" for the guilty person to void the test is much too good to pass up. If the suspect remains seated and tries to remain calm, he wants the test to work, indicating his innocence. If, however, he moves around, fidgets and the like, he is probably guilty. Remember, the guilty person wants to avoid an accurate reading while the innocent person wants the test to be as accurate as possible.

By gauging the suspect's real level of cooperation—how calm he tries to remain—you can determine his guilt or innocence quickly and with high certainty. Here's another example:

SNAP SHOT Cathy has been trying to get the neighbors to sign a petition allowing her to put up her holiday decorations in the small public area surrounding her community. While speaking to her neighbors, they all seem cooperative and supportive of her idea. But she's not so sure because the town board told her several neighbors had complained—and she has her suspicions the complainers include the Foley family. So, to find out if the Foleys are for or against her, she simply knocks on the door and says, "Here's the petition I need signed. I've got to run now, but if you can please leave it outside my door no later than 4:15 p.m., then I can return it on time."

Once they agree, she simply waits for what happens next. If they mysteriously "forget" or it's "blown away," they are clearly not for it. Of course, if they put up a reasonable resistance to bringing the petition across the street, it is possible they are not amongst her strongest supporters. If they place it by her door on time, it is probable they are for her campaign.

Technique 2: A Free Exchange

The person wanting to help you always needs information to be correctly exchanged. When he knows what you know and you know what he knows, he is in the best position to serve you. However, when he does not care to make sure you have all the facts or withholds some information, you know he's not fully, or even partially, committed to helping you and might be out to get you.

SNAP SHOT A co-worker says she will help you prepare for a meeting with a client. You aren't sure what her motivation is, so you put her to the test by baiting her with a bit of information she knows is not true and waiting to see if she corrects you. You would say something like, "Nancy, the client is looking for a campaign that's serious, but has some humor. They really like what we did for them last year, so I think we should do something along those same lines."

Now, the truth is that the clients have not been happy with the previous campaign and Nancy knows it. So, if she doesn't speak up, she's not for you; she wants to sabotage you.

So, the next time you want to find out whose side someone is really on, throw a misassumption—one she's sure to know isn't true and could be injurious to you—into the conversation, and notice whether or not she corrects you.

Technique 3: The Eager Beaver

In this technique, you can gauge a person's degree of loyalty by determining how agreeable he is under the specific set of circumstances. Now, the typical challenge is that the *saboteur appears* agreeable. You have to apply some tactful psychology. It works like this: you ask the person to give you something he can readily offer at no risk to himself. Then you turn up the heat a little by putting his personal interests in jeopardy. The technique has to be done in two steps.

SNAP SHOT You're a police officer canvassing a crime scene for witnesses. You approach a person you think saw exactly what happened. If you merely ask him, "Did you see anything?" and he responds by saying, "No" and proceeds to walk away, you are pretty much out of options. You still don't know if he saw something and is uncooperative, or if he's telling the truth.

Therefore, you will begin with an innocuous question, noting whether there is a *change in cooperation* and tone of conversation. For instance, you might say, "Do you feel comfortable living in this neighborhood?" or "Did you grow up around here?" You see, the questions are fairly non-threatening. Once you engage him in conversation with this harmless patter, you switch the focus and ask your main question: "Did you see what happened?" Now, if he says no and tries to walk off, you know he is an uncooperative witness who may know what happened but doesn't want to get involved.

However, if he says no but stays and continues to engage you in conservation, he is probably an ally and truly willing to help you. Of course, if at any time he acknowledges he saw something, you can assume there is a willingness to help. Take a look at another application:

SNAP SHOT A plant manager believes one of three unauthorized employees who have access to the warehouse looked through some confidential boxes. She says the following to the three suspects. "We know that a partial image of the thief was caught on camera (obviously not true, otherwise he would not need to interview them) and the company logo is missing from his jacket. Can I ask you three to bring your company jacket to my office?"

You have three people who presumably will be able to produce a jacket with logo intact. The real culprit is thrilled because he is able to offer "proof" that he is not guilty because his jacket is not missing a logo—in fact, *none of the jackets are.*

Now the technique takes a twist: when each employee comes to her with the jacket, she adds, "I was wrong, the camera did show a logo, but the image was very unclear so we didn't see it at first. So instead they want to test the jackets for traces of "warehouse dust"—you can leave yours with me now, or just drop it off before you leave work."

Now, she has him; the innocent person will leave the jacket in order to quickly clear his name. The guilty person wants to clean up the garment (likely offering a very poor excuse as to why he needs to take it with him) before he submits it for testing.

You see, if she initially asks the three men to turn in their jackets to be tested, she'll have no way of knowing who will be cleaning the jacket and who will drop it off without "tampering with the evidence." By informing her suspects of the new criterion, once the jackets are in her possession, she can readily tell who is cooperating and who isn't.

Technique 4: The Six-Star Test

In my book *Get Anyone to Do Anything*, I explored this very idea with a very simple test. In general, if you want to know if someone is a good friend, a fake or using you, try the following to see where her loyalty really lies:

Interest: One important criterion defining a friend is how interested the person is in your life. Tell her about something significant going on in your life and see if she calls to follow up and find out what happened. If she doesn't, call her and see if she mentions it. Finally, if she doesn't bring it up, drop a hint and see if she even remembers the previous conversation.

Loyalty: Tell a secret about a mutual friend and see if it gets back to her. True friends know the value of trust in a relationship. However, make sure you get your mutual friend's permission to tell her secret.

Pride: Anyone can tell you to "cheer up." It makes them feel good. But who pats you on the back for a good job? Friends not driven by envy will commend you. Your true friends are proud of your accomplishments, not jealous of your successes. Lots of people are willing to "cheer you up" when things aren't going well, but it's more difficult to find someone who will congratulate you when things are going well.

Honesty: A true friend tells you what you don't want to hear. She's willing to have you be upset with her, if it helps you. Does she tell you things for your benefit, though she knows it might make you upset with her?

Respect: Tell her there is something exciting going well in your life, but you absolutely prefer not to talk about it right now, and see if she presses you. There is a difference between curiosity and concern. If she "must know," she is interested in the gossip and not in you. A good friend respects your wishes and gives you your space—for now. She might bring it up from time to time, because she is interested, but she will not constantly and immediately press you on the subject if you have made it clear you choose not to discuss it now.

The reason you use a positive "mystery," and not a negative one, is that a good friend feeling something is wrong or that you are not well will insist on knowing now, because she is concerned. You don't want to "test" your friend this way, because you wouldn't want to worry her.

Sacrifice: Is she willing to give something up if it means making you happy? Will she sacrifice her own pleasure for your happiness? Who decides what you do together? Is the word "compromise" in her vocabulary? When the chips are down and it's you against them, most people scramble to protect personal interests. Notice if she's the one who has an idea or a plan to help both of you "escape unscathed," or she tries to save herself and protect her own interests.

It's very important to remember that all of us, at different times, become absorbed in our own lives and can't easily focus on someone else, even when we care deeply for them. Therefore, don't judge this person based on an isolated encounter, but rather over a good period of time.

Technique 5: The Big Sell

With this technique, you actually bring up your concern that she may not really be an ally. Then all you have to do is *gauge her mood*. After having been accused of such a disloyalty, the person, if really an ally, will still have some residual annoyance, sadness, or at least questions. However, if she is really a saboteur, she is eager to change the subject and you will notice a profound shift in mood—to *positive*—after this little talk.

The secret here lies not in gauging her mood while the subject is discussed, as she could be a convincing actress. Rather, once you move on, notice if she is pleased with herself for having "sold you," or upset with you for questioning her allegiance. The important part of the technique is to let her believe you accept what she says wholly and completely—no ifs, ands, or buts—so she doesn't believe she has to resell you, in which case it would appear that she is still annoyed.

SNAP SHOT You think a co-worker has been conspiring behind your back. Therefore, you simply bring up your concern in a non-threatening way. For instance, "Helen, I heard a rumor that you put Denise's promotion ahead of mine and downplayed my contribution to the team." Now, you pretty much ignore whatever she says. You smile and accept her response. Then take note if she continues to ask you "why" and "how" you could have thought the rumor implicates her, or if she disappears and heads to lunch. If she is truly an ally, she will want to set the record straight and clear the air. If she is a saboteur, she will try to end the conversation as quickly as possible.

> **QUICK TAKE** A person seeking to manipulate or control others almost always presents the image of a "helpful" person. Of course, he may simply be a good person, but you have to ask yourself the question, "Why is he being so nice to me?" Please understand, this is not to make a cynic out of you. Rather, it is a reminder that everyone has motivations—some good, and some bad. And if someone you don't know very well is being nice to you, especially if he does not seem to be in a good mood himself, it may be because he wants something from you and is getting ready to manipulate you.

Signal: Emotional Theft

Strong emotions cloud our perception of reality. More than 2,000 years ago, Aristotle had this to say about emotion and distortion: "Under the influence of strong feeling we are easily deceived. The coward, under the influence of fear, and the lover under that of love, have such illusions that the coward, owing to a trifling resemblance, thinks he sees an enemy, and the lover his beloved."

Emotional states are either self-induced, externally caused, or a combination of the two. Some of the more powerful ones include guilt, intimidation, appeal to ego, fear, curiosity, the desire to be liked, and love. When operating in any of these states, your judgment is likely to be impaired. Furthermore, anyone who uses any of these is attempting to move you from logic to emotion, in an attempt to manipulate you. In the process, the truth gets lost because you are not operating logically and cannot effectively see the evidence before you, let alone weigh it. Some generic examples of how manipulations sound are as follows:

SNAP SHOT **Guilt:** "How can you even say that? I'm hurt that you wouldn't trust me. I just don't know who you are anymore."

Fear: "You know, you might lose this entire deal. I don't think that's going to make your supervisor very happy. I hope you know what you're doing. I'm telling you that you won't get a better deal anywhere else. You're a fool if you think otherwise."

Appeal to Ego: "I see you're a smart person. I wouldn't try to put anything past you. You'd be on to me in a second."

Curiosity: "You only live once. Try it. You can always go back to how things were before. It might be fun—a real adventure."

Desire to be Liked: "I thought you were a real player. So did everybody else. It's going to be disappointing if you don't come through for us."

Love: "If you loved me, you wouldn't question me. I have only your best interest at heart. You know I wouldn't lie to you."

Look and listen objectively not only to the words but also the message. These manipulative factors hinder your ability to digest the facts. When emotions creep into your thinking, temporarily suspend your feelings and look in front of you, not inside yourself.

QUICK TAKE In *Living Without Conscience* (1999), Robert Hare warns us not to be influenced by "props"– the winning smile, the promises, the fast talk, and the gifts meant to deflect you from the manipulation and exploitation that may be occurring. "Any of these characteristics," he writes, " can have enormous sleight-of-hand value, serving to distract you from the individual's real message." You must look at the situation as objectively as possible, by seeing clearly what is happening versus the story being sold.

Emotional Profile: Learn Just How Safe, Stable, and Sane a Person Is

CHAPTER 7

"Ordinarily he was insane, but he had lucid moments when he was merely stupid."
Heinrich Helne (1 7 9 7 - 1 8 5 6)

Through casual observation or a two-minute conversation, you can learn the warning signs of emotional instability and the potential for violence. From a blind date, to the baby sitter, to a co-worker, gain the advantage by knowing what to look for and what questions to ask in order to protect yourself and your loved ones.

To fully understand the process of gauging someone's psychological welfare, we will walk through the internal forces and struggles each of us face, ultimately determining our degree of emotional well-being. We will also crystallize the general psychological process into clear, specific red flags you need to be on the lookout for.

What Makes a Person "Normal" or Not?

Within human beings, three inner forces exist, often at odds with each other: the soul (our conscience), the ego, and the body. The soul seeks to do what is right; the ego (or lower soul) wants to be right; and the body just wants to escape from all of it.

Doing what is easy or comfortable is a body drive. Examples of overindulgences of this drive are overeating or oversleeping—in effect, doing or not doing something we know we should or should not do, merely because of how it feels.

An ego drive can run the gamut from making a joke at someone else's expense to buying a flashy car that's beyond our means. In essence, this is doing something to appear a certain way to others. When we are driven by ego, we do things that we believe project the right image. These choices are not based on what is good but on what makes us look good.

Finally, a soul choice involves doing what is right, regardless of what we feel like doing.

In short, the body wants to do what feels good; the ego wants to do what looks good; and the soul wants to do what is good. When the alarm clock sounds in the morning, they all battle it out. If we hit the snooze button, guess who won the first round?

True freedom is not about being able to do whatever we feel like doing; rather, it is about being able to do what we truly want to do, in spite of what we feel like doing at the moment.

QUICK TAKE Imagine you are on a diet and suddenly feel like eating a piece of chocolate. You try hard to fight the temptation, but you can no longer resist; you cave in. Can it be said you are free? You felt like eating it, and you did. Is this freedom, or slavery? How do you feel afterwards? How will you feel about yourself if you resist the temptation?

When we rise above our inclinations and resist, we are exercising self-control. Only when we are *able* to choose responsibly, *and do so,* do we gain self-esteem. *Self-esteem and self-control are intertwined.* If we cannot control ourselves and give in to immediate gratification or live to promote and protect an image, we wind up feeling lousy. We are living at the whims of our own out-of-control impulses and dependent upon others to feed our self-image.

When we oversleep or overeat, we become angry with ourselves. On a deeper, often unconscious level, when we do things "for show," we feel empty inside. Our actions eat away at our self-esteem because we sacrificed the very thing we wanted—what was right for us to do—for the sake of an image.

Such a person is constantly angry and frustrated at life for coming up short. His expectations are never met. He is not complete and like a parasite, he feeds on almost anything—a passing compliment, control, power, even fear—and continually takes, rarely resisting the chance to impress. He is consumed with what he lacks, what he is owed, and what else he needs in order to be complete. He is endlessly searching because his quest is never satisfied: he is forever one more thing away from happiness.

The psyche of the self-absorbed person is ransacked by desires, fleeting impulses and urges twisting and pulling on his thoughts. When he is alone, in order to quiet the unconscious gnawing that says, "I don't like me," he does whatever he can to feel good.

This cycle spirals downward, because a person who does not feel good about himself often seeks the temporary, hollow refuge of immediate gratification and gives in to impulses instead of rising above them. The vapor-like pleasure masking his contempt for himself quickly dissipates because the comfort sought is replaced by greater pain. He only cycles lower and lower.

When we don't like who we are, more than not investing in ourselves, we punish ourselves in ways disguised as pleasure:

excessive eating, alcohol and drug abuse, and endless distractions to keep us from examining our lives. We want to love ourselves but lose ourselves instead. We are unable to invest in our well-being, so we substitute illusions for love.

QUICK TAKE Have you ever chatted pleasantly with someone whom you did not like very much? How about spending an hour or an entire day with someone who got on your nerves but to whom you had to be polite, responsive, and offer utmost respect? It's almost painful. What if you lived with that person… and that person was you? No matter what you did to distract yourself from yourself, you would be completely emotionally and physically drained.

The self-absorbed person doesn't like who he has become, so everything in life is hard. The effort is like working for a boss you can't stand. Even the most minor task is cause for frustration and angst. Would you work hard for or invest in, let alone love and respect, an ungrateful, out-of-control, arrogant person? You might try to quiet or distract him with pointless pursuits, or endless entertainment, or even help him get lost in a haze of alcohol—anything to keep you from having to face or deal with him.

When a person has no self-respect, he can't truly love himself. To fill the emotional void, he turns to the world for approval. This concept illuminates the source of all negative emotions, as well as interpersonal conflicts: the acceptance and recognition he craves comes in the package of respect. If the world respects him, then he can respect himself, converting their adoration and praise into self-love. His self-worth becomes a direct reflection of others' opinions. His mood is raw and he is vulnerable to every fleeting glance and passing comment.

The person who desperately needs to reclaim his sense of self-worth—through others—lives in a virtual feeding frenzy, always seeking attention and approval. *Anything* we do depending on others (for attention or approval) wears at us emotionally.

For example, if we dress for approval or make a decision to impress others, it makes us emotionally dependent. We put ourselves in a position of dependency and by extension, become more self-centered and vulnerable. And so we easily become neurotic, anxious, and even depressed. Think about this: if our self-worth is dependent upon others to feed us—with a nice word, we feel good; with a harsh glance, we feel bad—we are at the whim of the world to nourish us. Understand, though, that *we are never satiated.*

As we have said, we see our world through a distorted lens. Little reality comes through and what does can't be retained because we have no solid vessel to hold it.

QUICK TAKE   Imagine you are pouring water into a cup, but the cup has no bottom. As you pour in the liquid, the cup "feels" and looks full. As long as you are filling his cup, a dependent person is satisfied. But the minute you stop (the undivided attention, respect, or adoration), he is instantly empty and as thirsty as he was before. He can never be satisfied, no matter how much you give. The pouring offers an illusionary, fleeting satisfaction, flowing through him but never filling him. He desperately, constantly seeks love, approval, and respect from others but has no solid vessel to contain it. It flows out as fast as it is poured in.

Out of Control and Angry

By definition, low self-esteem means a person does not feel in control. Remember, self-respect comes from self-control, so any circumstance robbing him of his freedom takes away his last vestige of control. In effect, it harms his sole source of self-esteem and causes him to lash out. He is at the mercy of the world to make him feel good, so he fights, defending his ego and justifying his beliefs, values, and actions, as well as his right to be heard. He already feels out of control, so he will defend every last drop of true freedom he can maintain.

In the person who feels disrespected or out of control, a lack of self-respect causes an out-of-proportion response to any situation. The world, funneled through his ego, is his only source of psychological nourishment. When he feels he is not getting the respect he craves, anger—the ego's ultimate weapon—engages as a defense mechanism against feelings of vulnerability. Spiraling further and further from emotional health, he does not understand that the angrier he is, the less in control he becomes.

Some people direct anger outward and become mean, loud, and obnoxious, while others direct it inward and become perpetual doormats, trying to please the world in an attempt to gain love and appreciation. (We will discuss the implications and signs of the two types in the following chapters).

Okay—he has low self-esteem and is emotionally uneven. But does that mean he will become violent? No. However, the emotional groundwork has been laid, so the potential exists. Here are some strong signs of the potential for violence that you should be aware of, divided into three main sections:

I: General Signs Indicating the Potential for Violence
II: Romantic/Casual Encounters
III: Workplace: Are You in Danger?

I: Red Flags Indicating the Potential for Violence

In addition to the previous discussion on the psychology involved, look for the following signs that may indicate an increased likelihood of violence:

- How does he talk about his childhood, parents, siblings, other relatives, childhood friends, and so on? A person who speaks harshly about his childhood or relatives, using strong, perhaps violent language, clearly has unresolved issues that could lead to explosive consequences.

- Has he ever been abused? Robert Ressler, the FBI behavioral scientist who coined the term "serial killer," states in Whoever Fights Monsters (1993) that a startling 100 percent of serial killers have been abused as children by way of violence, neglect, or humiliation. We are not suggesting that a victim of abuse will become an abuser, but statically speaking, it is more likely that he will hurt another person because he was a victim himself.

- Does he tend to use force or violence in an attempt to resolve challenges? Will the person walk away from a fight or try to defuse it verbally, as opposed to resorting to physical conflict?

- Does he overreact to little things and assume a personal motivation? For instance, after the cashier gives him the wrong change or someone gives him poor directions, does he becomes enraged, believing the motivation was intentional and personal?

- Is he cruel to animals, or for that matter, people? Does he say hurtful things or seek to embarrass or humiliate others, particularly those who cannot easily defend themselves?

- Does he drink excessively, use other drugs, or engage in any risk-taking behavior without little regard for his own or others' safety and welfare?

This list isn't exhaustive and doesn't cover every possible scenario, but it sheds light on whether someone has the potential for becoming violent. Of course, if he has detailed plans to commit acts of violence, speaks about settling debts or getting respect, and has easy access to a weapon, you can be fairly sure violence may be imminent. Appropriate authorities should be contacted immediately, because someone's safety may be in danger.

II: Red Flags in Romantic/Casual Encounters

In addition to our previous analysis of signs of general violence, use the following red flags to determine if a potential companion may eventually cause you harm or become the partner from hell:

- A little jealously may be sweet—too much is poison. Jealousy has less to do with how a person feels towards you and more to do with how he feels about himself. It is an unhealthy emotion rooted in insecurity. Does he keep tabs on you and want to know where you are at all times? If he is jealous of others, as well as your friends and family, accusing you of flirting and trying to limit your activities when he is not involved, be aware. Furthermore, if he tries to restrict or control your time with friends and family, you're headed for a very serious problem.

- Are you scared in any way? Does he threaten you, or are you concerned about what he would do if you broke up with him? Does he ever, under the guise of joking, say something like, "I could never live without you and you wouldn't live either." Similar comments are not loving; they are cause for concern.

- Watch out for the two-faced person; if his personality is inconsistent, be on alert. He may act nicely to you and poorly to others. Of course, if he treats you poorly and is nice to others, you already know you have a problem. But the former is a concern because he is adjusting his conduct toward you for his own gain; his behavior is not a reflection of his true nature. How he treats others when he does not need anything from them is a stronger indicator of a core personality. Pay attention to how he regards people he does not "need" to be nice to, such as the waitress, a receptionist, or a doorman. These inter-actions are good indicators of his real character.

- If he is verbally abusive in any way, you should be advised physical abuse is statistically not far behind. While it may remain as verbal, the odds aren't in your favor.

- In the beginning of the relationship, did he come on too strong or too fast and become preoccupied with you and everything about you? While you may be flattered, you should be concerned. He doesn't have a realistic outlook about the relationship and is placing far more emphasis and attention than is warranted for a new rela-tionship. His behavior is indicative of a person who's not seeing reality very clearly.

- Have your friends or family told you that they do not like him or said that there "is just something about him" they don't quite like but can't put a finger on? If so, you may have lost perspective. Take a step back and look at the relationship as objectively as you can. Try taking a few days apart; go out of town if you can, and see if you are missing something you should be paying attention to in the relationship.

QUICK TAKE Gavin Debecker, noted security consultant in *The Gift of Fear* (1997), tells us not hearing the word "no" in any way shape or form is a very strong sign you may be in danger. Debecker says, when someone ignores you saying "no," he is seeking control of the situation or refusing to relinquish control. Do not negotiate with the person. "No" means "No." Remember, "No" is a complete sentence.

The previous red flags will let you know if you need to be aware of certain behavior. However, if he currently treats you roughly, regardless of any excuse he offers (or those that you offer for him!)—drinking, upset, having trouble at work, going through a difficult time, it will not happen again, and so on—*get out*, until he gets help.

III: Red Flags of Workplace Danger

Use the red flags in the previous two categories in addition to the red flags listed below to determine whether or not a person may be a danger to you in the workplace.

- Is he a loner, hypersensitive, or does he have difficult relationships with co-workers? A person who doesn't get along well with anyone may be harmless, but he can also be dangerous. Either way, be alert, particularly if he has a penchant for violence as illuminated in the previous two sections.

- Has he had a recent financial or personal crisis, such as a bankruptcy, separation, divorce, restraining order, custody battle, or hearing, and so on? Any significant negative shift in his life or lifestyle, combined with other factors, may be cause for concern.

- Is he not moving up the corporate ladder and showing frustration with his lack of progress? Or for that matter, does he remain suspended, passed over for promotions or advancement? If he seems particularly frustrated by work and unable to handle what he considers unfair and unjust, again, pay attention; it may be nothing, or it may be something.

- Has there been a sudden decline in workplace attitude, performance, or behavior? Does he suddenly seem disinterested and unaffected by the goings on at work? If so, look for the presence of the other signs in this and the previous two sections.

These warning signs should give you a "heads up" for any pending awareness issues. However, if he talks at all about being "fed-up" or "sick and tired" of "everyone and everything" or generally about a plan to get even or solve his problems, be on high alert.

In addition to the previous red flags, please read on to learn more about low self-esteem and other signs of possible abusive or violent behavior.

SECTION II

BLUEPRINTS TO THE MIND: UNDERSTANDING THE DECISION-MAKING PROCESS

Go beyond reading basic thoughts and feelings: Learn how people think so you can profile anyone, predict behavior, and understand a person better than he does himself.

- S.N.A.P. Isn't Based on Personality Type
- The Primary Colors of Thought
- How and Why We Think What We Do
- The Impact of Self-esteem: The Big Six
- Does He Have High Self-esteem, or Is He Just Pretending?
- The Self-Esteem Detector
- Three-Type Profile
- The Art and Science of Profiling: Real-Life Examples

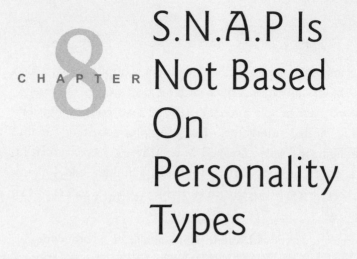

CHAPTER 8

S.N.A.P Is Not Based On Personality Types

"Personality can open doors, but only character can keep them open."

Elmer G. Letterman

Personality-typing has many practical applications; it also has its limitations. Even with the best system, the categories we place people into can often be time-consuming, confusing, and contradictory. For example, according to one paradigm, the well-respected Myers-Briggs, a person can be categorized as Introverted, Intuitive, Thinking and Judging (or INTJ for short). Here's a short blurb on one aspect of this type:

> Sensing serves with a good will, or not at all. As other inferior functions, it has only a rudimentary awareness of context, amount, or degree. Thus INTJs sweat the details or, at times, omit them. "I've made up my mind, don't confuse me with the facts," could well have been said by an INTJ on a mission. Sensing's extraverted attitude is evident in this type's bent-to-savor sensations, rather than to merely categorize them. Indiscretions of indulgence are likely an expression of the unconscious vengeance of the inferior.

Personality typing can be a highly effective tool, and conclusions may be drawn that the person you are speaking to is, for instance, detail-oriented. But even under the best circumstances, you still can't predict what the person is thinking in a specific instance.

Our personality is basically an interface between the world and us, and how we relate. But, because both the person and his world are in a constant state of flux, it can be difficult to get a consistently accurate read using personality-typing. For example, in different environments, the same person can exhibit varying personas. At work, he can be driven and demanding; at a dinner with friends, relaxed and accommodating; and around family, insane. Circumstances bring out different aspects of a person's integrated personality. A *split-personality*, by the way, occurs when aspects of the self are not integrated and each persona takes on a life of its own—hence the phrase "split-personality."

The same person can also act differently at different times within the same circumstance, because attitude and behavior also depend upon mood or the current state of mind, which is constantly shifting, regardless of personality.

As we know in our own lives, a shift in mood can dramatically alter how we see and feel about the current situation and ourselves. For instance, common sense (supported by studies) shows individuals in a depressed mood have less interest in social interaction and conversation. (Interesting and counter-intuitive, a person in a positive mood takes fewer risks than a person in a negative state—because he is more sensitive to loss). For example, a "Type-A" extrovert personality who is in a bad mood while at a party may act like an introvert.

Another relevant detail is that what we know about the situation can affect our attitude and decision-making process. Continuing with the above scenario, she can later be in a great mood and desire to meet Mr. X. However, if she knows coming on too strong will turn him off, she may alter her behavior.

We find that unchanging, universal, and overriding forces of human nature *direct* one's personality. S.N.A.P. uses the components of these forces to give us an accurate, predictable read of a person almost every time, in every unique situation.

The Primary Colors Of Thought

"Discovery consists of seeing what everybody has seen and thinking what nobody has thought."
Albert von Szent-Gyorgyi (1893 - 1986)

Now we see something truly amazing. The previous chapters give us a good insight into different aspects of a person's psyche for basic profiling and situation-gauging when only specific information is needed. This insight would be useful in a negotiation, to see if the person is confident; or on a date, to see if someone is interested. From this point, we take a more holistic approach to obtain a more complete understanding of our subject.

The system will help you to better understand how and why a person thinks the way he does, and to better predict what he will do in a given situation. Human nature is the hardware running the program we call "thought"—input in, input out. It does the same thing every time, based upon the commands entered. Although rarely simple, it is an equation nonetheless, once you understand the psychology behind the commands.

You can tell what someone is thinking because, in reality, he's not thinking. Outside of real creative thought, human beings are actually forced into conclusions about how and what they see. What often passes for thought is really a response based on *emotionally* pre-programmed choices. (We are not speaking of a logical decision that, while it incorporates emotions, continues to remain a free-will choice, whereby two people with the same "input" respond with differing behavior).

Specifically, statistically speaking, a woman who is highly promiscuous and engaged in rampant, casual sex or prostitution was probably sexually abused, in some fashion, as a girl or young adult. In fact, studies show, more than 75 percent of teenage prostitutes have been sexually abused.

So, what's going on here? In order to reconcile and make sense of what happened to her, she is forced, albeit unconsciously, to reduce the significance of the event. By diluting the value and sanctity of sexual relations, her willful promiscuity makes what happened to her seem less significant and less important. Simply put, the value of what was harmed, or taken from her, has been reduced.

Otherwise, she is forced to reconcile something much more traumatic. To reduce the emotional pain of dissonance, she engages in a self-destructive lifestyle. Devaluing sexual activity, diluting it to the point of insignificance, reinforces her belief that it does not matter.

Therefore, if you can tell, through quick observation, that she was a victim of abuse, you know more about her thoughts on men, sex, and herself than she does. In addition, you will know this, not because of her personality, but based on human nature.

Consider another example. You're wearing a brand-new, very expensive suit. In speaking with a colleague, she remarks it is the most gorgeous and beautifully crafted suit she has ever seen. You think this person knows quality, so you'll simply say "thank you" or possibly tell her the cost. However, if she has learned the price, and tells you she thinks you overpaid, you will believe she doesn't know a thing about quality. Furthermore, you may inform her of the hand-stitched craftsmanship and how the suit will keep shapely and last for years to come.

The difference in your attitude and response is pre-programmed. When a person's ego (which is emotionally charged) is engaged, he feels psychologically threatened and his thoughts go into "self-defense" mode. The applicable force of nature is effectively illustrated in the great American pastime called gambling.

> **QUICK TAKE** We literally are almost always "forced" into our attitudes and thoughts based upon specific forces of human nature. In an interview conducted by Robert Anton Wilson, self-styled guru of human motivation, Dr. Ernest Dichter was asked about his use of psychology in advertising. He declared, "Nobody is invulnerable. Ninety-nine percent of human actions are irrational. I buy more useless things than the rest of my family put together."

Casinos work on a percentage of as little as two percent for some games like blackjack and baccarat; in some instances, the margin can be as low as 1.17 percent. So why, on a typical day, do more than 85 percent of gamblers walk away losers?

Look at the stock market. It can move in one of two directions: up or down. Conventional wisdom suggests you have a "fifty-fifty" chance of winning or losing. Yet, (statistics vary on this), roughly 77 to 95 percent of people who play the market daily—by themselves, without outside input—will, over time, lose. Why? Not because of the odds, but because of human nature. Let's better understand the psychology at work with two basic, distinct styles of play:

Gambler A: The Chaser

Here's a typical scenario: a person bets $10 and loses; he then bets $10 again and loses. Next, he bets $20 and loses, then $30 and again loses. *He increases his bets as he does worse.* The gambler tries to chance his money—trying to win it all back in one hand by betting more to make up for the times he lost. When a person's ego is engaged, he will be inclined to chase.

Gambler B: The Chased

Here's a typical scenario for this mentality: a person bets $10 and loses; he bets $10 and loses again. After some time, his bet shrinks to $5. Good plan? Possibly not. If he wins, he feels he should have bet more and if he loses, he still lost. He is partly pleased that he lost, because only through losing can he now justify to himself lowering his bet! Again, the ego is lurking.

Interestingly, people with LE-D profiles (we will discuss shortly in Chapter 14 what this means) will likely engage in behavior B ("the chased") while individuals with LE-A profiles will often pursue behavior A ("the chaser"). A person with higher self-esteem may do either, but will temper his play with better judgment and objectivity.

> **QUICK TAKE** In situations having temporary conse-
> quences, where little or no effort or inher-
> ent interest is involved, a person's actions can be completely
> orchestrated merely by a suggestion that instantly, albeit tem-
> porarily, reshapes his self-concept (via the ego). For instance,
> you want a co-worker to sign a petition. You might say, "You
> know Gary, I always appreciated the fact that you're some-
> one who is willing to get behind a good cause or idea." Once
> Gary thanks you for your kind words, he has unconsciously
> virtually locked-in to signing the petition, should you ask
> within a few minutes time.

The ego is irrational, but irrational does not mean unpre-
dictable. If you know what elements are in play, you can
readily know what the person's feelings and attitudes are
toward you and the situation. So what are the elements? Take
a look:

The Primary Colors

From the three primary colors—red, blue, and
yellow—you can create millions of distinct and discernable
colors. For instance, mixing blue and red makes purple,
yellow and red makes orange, and yellow and blue makes
green.

Similarly, when you understand the primary colors of the
mind, all you need to know is how much of each "color" is
present to tell the "shade" of the person's thoughts within a
situation. In painting, temperature, color saturation and brush
type, among other things, alter the paint formula in subtle

ways. So, there are secondary factors influencing our thinking, which we will discuss as well. Following is a brief outline, and then a deeper exploration of how the factors direct our thoughts:

The Three Primary and Four Secondary Factors

Self-esteem—the degree to which a person likes himself and feels worthy of happiness.

Confidence or Self-efficacy—the degree to which a person feels competent and effective, within the given situation.

Level of Interest—what exactly is at stake, or the degree to which one cares about the conversation or situation.

We will examine other psychological variables which influence, to varying degrees, the thought and decision-making process: effort, justification, beliefs, and mood.

Effort—how much work, emotional, physical, financial, and so on, is necessary to achieve the objective.

Justification and Rationalization—to make sense of our previous behavior, a person builds a vision of himself and his world that may be slightly, or very inconsistent with reality—he then seeks to perpetuate this image.

Beliefs—anything a person holds to be true, whether or not it is consistent with the facts.

Mood—a person's current state of mind, as it relates to his circumstances.

Now we'll delve into the psychology behind the formula so you can see exactly how a person comes to behave the way he does. With this understanding, you can more effectively determine what a person is thinking and how he may respond to any new situation or circumstance.

10

How And Why We Think What We Do

"There is no expedient to which a man will not go to avoid the labor of thinking."

Thomas A. Edison (1847-1931)

elf-esteem literally translates to self-love; it simply refers to how much a person likes himself. As we will see, self-esteem is the master primary color, because it is the filter determining how much of the real world comes in and how much we distort via the ego. In the next few chapters, we'll explore the psychology in great depth because of its overriding significance.

The system in this section is not so much about techniques; it's about understanding fundamental components of a person's psyche. Once you understand the master template, you'll be able to use your knowledge in any situation you choose.

Self-Esteem and the Ego

In Chapter 7, we discussed the process by which we gain self-esteem and how it colors our perspective. Briefly, when we overcome the urge to do what is easy, and instead do what is right, we feel good about ourselves. Thus, we gain self-respect and self-esteem.

The ego and self-esteem are generally inversely related. The greater the self-esteem, the smaller the ego. Less "us" remains in the picture, and we see reality more clearly, because the ego distorts the clarity of our perspective. So, if we know how big his ego is, we can tell exactly what he's forced to see.

The Power of Perspective

The word "ego" is bandied about with ambiguous abandon. In a nutshell, it's the glue bonding our self-concept to our beliefs, values, and behaviors. It seeks consistency and permanence, regardless of whether it is in our best interest. Otherwise, we would simply change our behavior based on rational information. We would exercise and eat healthy to feel better, apologize and make up, even when we were right, or admit we made a huge mistake to someone always finding fault with us. The ego is what stops us. Therefore, knowing how "big an ego" someone has is crucial to gaining insight into his way of thinking.

The ego filters our world, keeping out what harms, or even causes deviation in how we need to see ourselves, and how we insist others see us. Our ego colors the world, so we remain untainted. We saw examples earlier: remember the promiscuous girl and the expensive suit? Now, let us delve into the psychological mechanics behind this aspect of human nature.

Bill buys a watch for $500. He flips through a magazine and sees what seems to be the same watch advertised for $300, producing an emotional inconsistency. He wants to see himself as a smart guy and savvy shopper, yet the ad suggests evidence to the contrary. Either he was duped and overpaid or the advertisement is not what it appears to be.

Bill's level of self-esteem determines his thought process. Higher self-esteem means he'll see the ad and not quickly flip the page. He'll read it and, if he believes it to be accurate, conclude he made a mistake. With lower self-esteem, Bill may fall back into a belief system saying the whole world is crooked and no one gets a fair shake, not even someone as savvy as himself. In this case, he deflects the damage away from his ego. He may also realign values and decide quickly, before his conscious mind is forced to accept an unpleasant reality, that time is more important than money and it simply isn't worth it.

If a person lacks self-esteem, he does not look to himself. He can't afford to be wrong emotionally or to see himself, or have the world see him, as less. So instead of changing who he is, he changes his view of the world, bringing order from chaos without ever damaging a hair on his emotionally volatile head. The thought "I am bad, or wrong" is replaced by "the world is unfair," "she is wrong," or "people are out to get me."

In extreme instances, if a person can't come to grips with his reality, meaning he's unwilling or unable to consciously feel guilt and remorse, he unconsciously resorts to changing his perception of events. A man cheating on his wife, for instance, has to justify his behavior. If he can't contort his world enough by reshaping his beliefs about his wife and marriage, or realigning his values to justify his behavior, he will engage in distortion of reality. This distortion causes him to "see" his wife doing things wrong and to unconsciously root for her to give him retroactive justification for his behavior.

DAVID J. LIEBERMAN

> **QUICK TAKE** A leading white-collar criminal defense attorney once remarked that his hardest job is convincing his client he has done something wrong. It is so easy to get caught up in the activity and justify every little step. Without realizing it, you have moved a great deal in a very wrong direction. Most people recognize that robbing, murdering, and hurting others is wrong. But in the area of accounting, for example, with no tangible victim and armed with "reasonable rationalizations," a person can be blinded to the impact of his actions.

Predicting the Path

Thus far, we see a person with high self-esteem will more clearly evaluate information while someone with lower self-esteem is forced to bend his thinking to follow the course of least resistance.

Dissonance forces a person to reconcile the discrepancy and reduce pain. For instance, a person with low self-esteem cannot usually admit to himself that he may have made a mistake. *Being right* becomes more of an emotional priority than *doing what is right*.

A person's instinct is to protect the psychological self, in much the same way, you protect your physical self. As you will go to great lengths to protect your body from harm, you also seek to protect your self-image. When your physical self is threatened, you engage in what is referred to as the "fight-or-flight" response. Similarly, when your psychological self is threatened, the mind engages in what is called the "accept-or-deflect" response. When a self-image is healthy and strong, a challenge to the self is usually accepted and confronted. When the self-image is weak, the ego protects itself by distorting the world, to avoid being injured. If you know how much reality is getting in, then you know a great deal about what a person sees to be true.

If a person's level of self-esteem is so crucial to gauging his thought process, the million-dollar question becomes, how do you tell how much a person "likes" himself?

First, we'll briefly see how self-esteem impacts the other colors (and offers us ways to gauge a person's self-esteem). Then, we'll learn a clear-cut, readily observable method of determining how a person truly feels about himself, without even engaging him in conversation.

CHAPTER 11

The Impact Of Self-esteem: The Big Six

"The nice thing about egotists is that they don't talk about other people."

Lucille S. Harpern

elf-esteem affects the other two colors, as well as the four additional variables. It's the most influential factor determining thought and action. Two people with theoretical 100 percent self-esteem will almost always make the same decision—to do what they believe is right (what they believe is right will vary, but not as much as you might think).

Everything we experience shapes us—either by adding to self-esteem or subtracting from it. As we put our colors into the mix, we see the practical, real-world, overriding influence of self-esteem on a person's thinking and decision-making processes. We will now see the impact in six areas: type of interest, confidence, effort, beliefs, justification, and mood.

Factor 1: Type of Interest

An overweight, diabetic woman knows she shouldn't be eating chocolate cake for dinner, but eats it anyway. Of course, it's not in her best interest, but because of low self-esteem, her interests change. Lying on the couch eating cheese doodles is undoubtedly pleasurable, yet most people do not spend all day indulging. Different types of interest are sought and dictated by a person's self-esteem. When self-esteem is low, the type of interest shifts to the now: A person will find appealing that which centers on his needs and offers more immediate satisfaction—be it for ego or physical desires.

Someone who has low self-esteem is emotionally immature and is primarily interested in the here and now, often forsaking his long-term self. He most certainly can't focus on another's satisfaction and pleasure unless there is an ulterior, selfish motive. When self-esteem increases, his interest level rises to that which offers longer-term satisfaction. He finds pleasure in more meaningful things benefitting him down the road, at the expense of immediate gratification.

The graph shown here is psychologist Abraham Maslow's *Hierarchy of Needs*, a schema showing the different levels of needs that human beings seek. At the bottom are the most

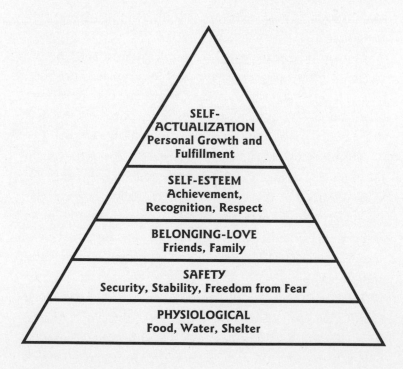

basic needs necessary for survival. As each need is met, we strive higher to greater emotional fulfillment.

Generally speaking, at the top rung the person is most flexible, honest, and open. He operates with a higher degree of intellectual integrity. As we move down the pyramid, emotions play a stronger role in the decision-making process. Increasingly, the person's needs take center stage, and his focus shifts from outward to inward. His perspective narrows as his ego looms larger, seeking to satisfy his own desires at the expense of what is possibly right or more right.

Very much like our single-celled friend, the amoeba, we are inclined to move toward pleasure and away from pain. The exact things, however, that we link pleasure or pain to vary from person to person.

Human beings are wired to be pleasure seekers. By the nature of reality, pleasure is attached to meaning. Therefore, when we do what is right—and seek meaning over temporary gratification—we gain pleasure; when we do not, we feel depressed, anxious and suffer from poor relationships.

The pleasure/pain mechanism is what keeps us moving in the right direction. In order for free-will to exist, the illusion—fortified by the ego—has to be equally as attractive as the reality. As we know, the less ego someone has the more reality he sees. Thus, he makes better choices because he can see clearly what's in his best interest and is more meaningful and pleasurable.

Low self-esteem is the force behind the impulse that causes a person to satiate the appetites of the ego and body. Because we are designed to seek pleasure, when we don't obtain it in reality through connecting to meaning, we seek pleasure through fleeting outlets. We often deceive ourselves

DAVID J. LIEBERMAN

into believing what we are doing is important, so we can still pursue what is fun, yet gain a feeling of relevance. We slap meaning onto nonsense, telling ourselves and others that what we're doing has significance, when we know deep down that we're seeking to justify the continuity of our actions.

For instance, how would you feel if someone pulled a few strings to get you a great job? You would probably feel pretty good. How might you feel if you found out after thirty years on the job, that everything was fake; that you had pushed buttons not attached to any working machine and your phone had rung to actors who were merely playing along. In fact, you were wildly successful at your "job," but none of it was real. Most people would be devastated—but why? The answer is simple: your work was not real and had no meaning, therefore was not pleasurable.

The more engaged in life you are, the more meaningful and thus pleasurable your experiences will be. The more you withdraw into temporary comfort or pursue illusions driven by the ego, the less pleasurable life becomes. In this state, you sometimes feel productive, but deep down inside recognize that your pursuits are not fulfilling. No matter how much effort you expend, the satisfaction is fleeting because the end objective is not meaningful. Being comfortable and having fun are not enough; our soul gnaws at us, not just to do more, but also to become something more.

It's abundantly clear how important it is to know whether a person has high or low self-esteem, and to see what he will be interested in and likely will pursue. Let's continue briefly exploring the other factors self-esteem impacts.

Factor 2: Confidence

People with higher self-esteem have greater confidence in their ability to think and act effectively, particularly in new situations. They can persevere more easily when faced with difficult challenges and are not consumed with the possibility of failure. Remember, the less self-esteem a person has, the greater his ego and the greater his concern with what others may think of him, as well as his own preoccupation with performance.

Factor 3: Effort

A person wants to do something, but if it is not worth the effort, he will not take action—no surprise here. What is newsworthy, however, is that the effort required impacts not only our decision to take action or not but also *changes how we think and feel about the situation.* Why is this so?

Imagine a person knows he should help a friend but simply doesn't feel like it. He may justify not helping by thinking the friend really does not need his help. He'll further rationalize not helping by thinking "he's not such a good friend anyway," or "I'm entitled to rest because I work very hard." Therefore, we must put into the equation the degree of effort, however we quantify it, to gain insight into his thinking as well as his possible next move.

Additionally, the absolute pain or effort involved is only measured in contrast to the level of self-esteem. The higher the esteem, the less the perceived effort. The pain we feel is inversely correlated to self-esteem.

For example, we may normally do almost anything for someone we love. But even the slightest effort is painful when we feel less appreciation from, or anger toward, the person. Then, most any effort is arduous. The reaction harkens back to us. People with higher self-esteem don't feel the effort or pain involved in doing what is right, in contrast to those with lower self-esteem.

When we love ourselves, we can invest in our long-term satisfaction and well-being with maximum effort and minimal pain. Even though we are expending a great deal of energy, self-esteem taps us into an unlimited source of energy and inspiration.

We can sum it up by saying the higher a person's self-esteem, the more willing he is to put effort into himself and his life and to do what is right when it concerns others.

Factor 4: Values and Beliefs

If you're dating someone you like and who likes you but you believe all women will hurt you, your interest level in her contradicts your motivation to act. Another example is this: if you believe a lie-detector test does not work, then it won't work on you. It will fail not because the test doesn't work but because it's predicated on the belief: if you lie, the machine will not know. So there is no fear, and that is what the machine measures.

Unhealthy or false beliefs are formed to protect us and are based on our limitations. Almost everything we do or believe is to justify our behavior to the world and ourselves. If we do not feel we need to hold onto a belief that is false or damaging, we can let it go. Self-esteem gives us the emotional fuel and the ability to release.

Narrow values are also built on low self-esteem. When we can't reach beyond our own wants and needs, we'll align our values to accommodate our narcissism. We lower the bar instead of raising our consciousness.

Factor 5: Justification and Rationalization

To reduce guilt, we have to make sense of our previous behavior. To feel better about ourselves in general, or things done to us, we build a vision of the world and ourselves that is consistent with what we need to be true, not with what is true.

> **QUICK TAKE** Fascinating research shows us an interesting relationship between reward and behavior. One such study found people who were paid $100 to perform a task rated it as more difficult and stressful than individuals paid $25 to perform the same task under identical conditions. We learn when a person is compensated for something, he often finds the task to be more difficult and less enjoyable, and as the size of the reward increases, his motivation and interest decline (Freedman, 1992). A person with higher self-esteem will have greater intellectually honesty, and so his thinking will be more congruent with reality.

When we choose to do something, if we aren't paid or otherwise compensated, we're unconsciously driven to like it more. Why else would we be doing it? We would prefer not to think we made a mistake. We must justify ourselves. The process, which is mostly unconscious, engages the ego. It warps the information process in a way that prevents us from seeing or thinking clearly about what is before us. Consider another example: an alcoholic, who works a dead-end job and is on his third marriage, can conclude either that he needs help or that the world is unfair. We need to know how he colors his world in order to get an accurate read on his thoughts and feelings in a given situation.

Justification also takes place in specific instances. If someone has invested a considerable amount of time, effort, energy, or money, then his outlook is similarly skewed. His ego makes it harder for him to walk away and will justify why it makes sense. If a person invests a great deal of time, the psychological phenomenon of cognitive dissonance is engaged and the person does not want to have to "lose" his investment. He is less able to take a "hit to the ego."

This particular human tendency is precisely why a car salesperson keeps you waiting for so long while he talks to the "sales manager." The more time you spend waiting, the harder it is to walk away. The same is true in dating. A person who has invested herself for a long time in a relationship is less likely to call it a day. Please understand, self-esteem is, again, the pivotal component used to evaluate the situation. Someone with low self-esteem won't believe he wastes his time, while someone with higher self-esteem is able to accept a situation, see it, and leave when it no longer makes sense. So while these factors, such as time invested, energy, and effort, are important to know, self-esteem is more influential as it dictates the weight of this emotional force.

Factor 6: The Mood Override

Mood is the shadow of self-esteem, temporarily lifting or deflating us, coloring how we see our world and ourselves. The lower a person's self-esteem, the more mood becomes a factor in his thinking and feelings. As stated, when a person has very low self-esteem, he is absorbed in himself. Therefore, his thoughts and actions are more likely to depend on his mood.

Since low self-esteem creates a looming ego, situations affecting others are not as important as they might be for someone who is more emotionally stable. When things do affect someone with low self-esteem, they are much more magnified. He is quick to assume everything is about him. What else can something be about than him, the center of the universe? Therefore, two factors determine the weight of mood on the decision-making process: self-esteem and the significance of the event. When classifying a person as having very low self-esteem and the situation is not of great significance, mood is a powerful force in the decision-making process.

For instance, a person may not be in the mood to take out the garbage (insignificant event), but if he has come home after being away for three weeks, and his fiancée's parents are coming over for the first time, whatever self-esteem he has will kick into high gear. A person may not be in the mood to call his sister to apologize after a big fight, but if she's sick and in the hospital, then self-esteem becomes the barometer. Let's also be clear that someone with higher self-esteem would not let the garbage pile up in the first place, nor would he let his ego dictate the relationship with his sister.

As we discussed earlier, when one's self-esteem is higher, he is more driven to do what's right, regardless of whether or not he feels like it. But as self-esteem lowers, his mood begins to dominate the thought process, with his subsequent behavior hinging upon the significance of the situation.

When the ego is engaged we cannot easily see or feel beyond our own pain. This is similar to physical pain whereby someone with a toothache, for instance, finds it difficult to focus on the needs of another. Feeling compassion for the hungry, homeless, and suffering becomes next to impossible with a throbbing tooth.

Having a greater understanding of self-esteem and the role it plays in a person's attitude, thoughts, and behavior is necessary to learn how to identify what people with high self-esteem look like and the counterfeits for whom they are often mistaken.

12

Does He Have Self-Esteem, Or Is He Just Pretending? The Five Pitfalls

---

"If you develop an ear for sounds that are musical, it is like developing an ego. You begin to refuse sounds that are not musical, and that way cut yourself off from a good deal of experience."

John Cage (1912 - 1992)

As we will see, evaluating a person's degree of self-esteem is not difficult, but can be tricky if you do not know what to pay attention to and what to ignore. Here are five main pitfalls to avoid in this process:

Pitfall 1: Self-Esteem Versus Ego

Don't fall into the trap of believing the person who has a big ego likes himself. We must remember that the ego and self-esteem are generally inversely related. No matter how much a person appears be happy with himself, if he has a big ego, he is not—he is miserable. The statement is not conjecture, but a law of human nature—it is psychological math. So insidious is this law, that a person may actually think he likes himself while his behavior betrays his real feelings.

Differentiating between self-esteem and ego can be difficult. For instance, take someone who plays his car radio loudly. Do we assume he has low self-esteem and craves attention, or does he have high self-esteem and simply not care what other people think of him?

And what about physical appearance? Somebody who's always well-dressed may suffer from low self-esteem and need others to think she is beautiful, put-together, and fashionable in order to feel good about herself. Or, she may have high self-esteem, and her attire is merely a reflection of her self-worth. Conversely, is someone who dresses sloppily doing so because he likes himself and does not care what others think? Or does he have such low self-esteem he does not care enough to look decent? You see the problem. The miscues are endless, and it gets even trickier.

For instance, it's too easy to say that someone who over-eats and does not take care of his health dislikes himself. Rather, the case may be that he has guilt over something specific, or perhaps has childhood issues specifically related to food. To a novice observer, the person may be labeled as having low self-worth when, in actuality, the contrary is true. Consider the opposite: perhaps a person gorges himself non-stop but has a fast metabolism. This person's appearance wouldn't reveal that he's an over-eater.

Pitfall 2: Self-Esteem Versus Confidence

How do you distinguish between self-esteem and confidence? As we suggested earlier, maybe the person is sure of himself in a given situation and appears to have all of the classic signs of high self-esteem. Conversely, a person may, in fact, have high self-esteem but in this instance he seems withdrawn, uneasy, and unsure. We can see that discerning between self-esteem and confidence can be problematic. But it's certainly necessary to accurately read a person.

Pitfall 3: The Success Story

We can't look at how successful a person is in order to gauge self-esteem, because society's idea of success may be very different from our own.

As we learned, choosing to do what is right—being free from the ego and over-indulgent body drives—gives us self-respect. Nowhere is this more evident than in a person's life in general. A person who does what he wants to do in life and isn't driven by ego or weighed down by immediate gratification, effectively gains self-esteem. Conversely, one who isn't doing what he wants, even if he is successful or is doing what he wants and is not where he thinks he "should" be in terms of progress, will suffer from low self-esteem.

For instance, a partner in a major law firm may be successful to the casual observer, but if he always wanted to be a musician and went into law to appease his father, he cannot, by psychological law, have high self-esteem because his decision was ruled by fear. Conversely, a poet with no money who enjoys writing for writing's sake can be full of self-esteem if he considers himself a success. Someone doing extraordinary things can feel depressed and suffer from low self-esteem if he hasn't achieved the level of success he aspires to because he's pursuing his objective for ego-based motivations and needs the accolades and praises of others.

Pitfall 4: Humility or Doormat?

It's easy to mistake humility for weakness; rather, it is strength. If a person is consumed with himself, he's arrogant, the opposite of being humble. An arrogant person only takes. He's an emotional junkie, depending upon others to feed his fragile ego, or a slave to his own impulses, which he can't rise above.

DAVID J. LIEBERMAN

When a person has humility, he is fulfilled. He is free to do *what is right* over that which merely makes him look good or is simply easy. Because humility allows us to choose to do what is right, it gives us self-control. This is the gateway to *self-esteem* and to emotional freedom.

The challenge here is obvious: how can you know if a person is merely "acting humble," when in fact, he's not doing good because he likes others, but needs for them to like him? Maybe he gives, not because he feels good, but because he is afraid to say no or does not feel worthy of asserting himself. Clearly, we need a way to separate those who really have self-esteem, and so humility, from those who allow themselves to become doormats.

Pitfall 5: Self-Esteem Versus Mood

As we also learned earlier, self-esteem determines how much mood becomes a factor in our profiling. Moreover, distinguishing between the two can be problematic, as mood can look a lot like self-esteem. Maybe the person is in a good mood, acts accordingly and sounds a lot like someone who is really comfortable in his own skin—outgoing, engaging, warm, considerate, and so on, but in actuality is a self-absorbed narcissist who for a short span of time merely adopts this persona. Do you see the problem?

Here's the good news: in the next chapter, you'll see there is only *one method* that is consistently effective in determining if a person has high or low self-esteem, without misreading or mislabeling his behaviors.

CHAPTER 13

The Self-Esteem Detector: Determining A Person's Level Of Self-Esteem

"*Self-esteem is the reputation we acquire with ourselves.*"

Dr. Nathaniel Branden

We explored the overall psychology to better help you to have greater flexibility in gauging someone's profile and to give you more options in what to look for and pay attention to. Because of the pitfalls we saw earlier, it is extremely difficult to tell whether or not someone has high self-esteem by using any one sign.

A person can be giving, but the question you have to ask yourself is, "why?" Is he doing it because he likes the other person or he wants the other person to like him? Does he seek to continuously improve and work on himself because he feels good about who he is or is he an overachiever compensating for feelings of insecurity? The miscues are endless.

How can you tell if someone has high self-esteem? *We see it as a reflection of how he treats himself and others.* A person who lacks self-esteem may indulge in things to satisfy only his own desires and will not treat others particularly well. Or, he may cater to others because he craves approval and respect, but he won't take care of his own needs. Only someone who truly has self-esteem will treat both himself and others well. When we say well, we don't mean engaging in short-term gratification; rather, he invests in his long-term well-being as well as being kind and good to others.

We might erroneously conclude that a person delaying gratification is engaging self-control and assume this is reflective of self-esteem. But unless we look at the other side of the coin, we are left with only half of a story. What if the person doesn't eat tasty, fattening foods (delayed gratification) so she can lose weight to attract a married man? We must see the full equation to see if the motivations balance out and produce self-esteem or not. This woman, for instance, would demonstrate cracks in her self-esteem because, as a matter of human design, she will treat others poorly.

CHAPTER 14 Three-Type Profile

"Creative powers can just as easily turn out to be destructive. It rests solely with the moral personality whether they apply themselves to good things or to bad. And if this is lacking, no teacher can supply it or take its place."

Carl Jung (1875 - 1961)

You can readily tell when a person has low self-esteem, but this may not automatically mean that he has a big ego. When self-esteem begins to erode, two distinct mentalities are produced. His perspective shrinks and more of his "personality" comes through, filtered by his unique insecurities. Two people with low self-esteem can manifest one of two different attitudes toward the same situation. From the two types, we can determine a person's general thinking, feelings, and overall attitude to any situation.

One can have a diminished ego and high esteem—this is the humble person; one can have a large ego and low self-esteem—this is the arrogant person. There is another possibility: one can have low esteem and a diminished ego—this is the doormat mentality. However, *one cannot have high self-esteem and a large ego.*

The person most dangerous to others is the one with the big ego and little or no self-esteem. The most dangerous to himself is one with a diminished ego and little self-esteem. The reason is an arrogant person is more likely to direct his anger outward. We see that violent criminals often have a certain bravado and smugness. A person without much ego and low self-esteem, however, is more inclined to direct negativity inward and blame himself for feelings of unworthiness. Let's gain a deeper clarity with these types.

LE-D Doormat: This person is quick to apologize, even when something is not her fault. She does things for others she doesn't really want to do, not because she likes them, but rather because she fears not being liked. She rarely stands up for herself, as she doesn't feel her needs are important enough and certainly not more important than others'. She is a quintessential people-pleaser. A person who "gives" to be liked can often, on the surface, be confused with one giving because it is the right thing to do or because she wants to give.

The same action will cause two distinct emotional imprints, based on your intention. It is the difference between being robbed and giving a donation. In both cases, money is going from you to another; but one instance is empowering, while the other is weakening. Accordingly, one enhances self-esteem while the other is emotionally draining. Please understand, if you give out of fear or guilt, this does nothing to enhance self-esteem; indeed, it only diminishes it. You aren't really giving; the other is person taking. You are being taken advantage of, with your consent. Only when you choose is free-will engaged and your sense of independence nourished.

You know in your own life, when someone tries to guilt you into doing something, you say "no," stand up for yourself and feel better about yourself. It is the same type of empowerment felt when you say "yes" to a request you should accommodate, even if you are not in the mood. Whatever you say or do, as long as it is from a position of strength—meaning you choose your course of action—you feel better. When you see yourself as incomplete, you allow yourself to be robbed to assuage feelings of inadequacy.

This profile most often produces a person who is introverted. When she is in her element, however, and feels comfortable and confident, she springs to life. While she is usually reserved, she often blossoms when she feels safe, secure, and in a good mood.

Signs of LE-D

Most people have some elements of each classifications, but generally speaking, these are the characteristics associated with an LE-D type:

- He doesn't accept compliments well.
- He's unassertive and doesn't speak up to defend himself.
- He speaks negatively about himself.
- He's constantly apologizing and feeling guilty.
- He suffers from an infinite variety of psychosomatic illnesses.
- He may be anxious and nervous when he's around new people or out of his comfort zone or environment, and prefers to stay where he feels safe.
- He fears taking even smart, calculated risks.

LE-A Arrogant

This person needs to be the center of attention and is often loud, easily frustrated, and a big complainer. His insistence of greatness masks the pain of low self-worth. He seeks constant reinforcement and adulation from others, and will become angry when these are not received in sufficient and continual quantities. He usually doesn't mind offending or insulting someone if it will make him look better or smarter in others' eyes.

He's often a fierce competitor whose self-worth hangs in the balance of every competition. He is controlling, narcissistic, self-absorbed, pushy, and full of bravado to compensate for feelings of inadequacy. When he gives his opinion, he is often offended if his ideas are not accepted. He insists people understand his point of view, despite a complete and sometimes obvious lack of interest; he merely sees this as stubbornness and the other person's own ego ignoring his always good advice. While a person with high self-esteem will be concerned about offending, embarrassing, or annoying other people, the LE-A person does not respect others, because he is largely unable. A person gives respect, so if he has none for himself, what is he giving? He actually—to varying degrees—lacks the capacity to give. Little room for others exists when his sense of self-importance drips into every relationship. A self-absorbed person has no capacity to love, as he only lusts when his ego is in control. Moreover, he is hyper-sensitive to criticism about himself, often responding with anger.

The more accepting we are of ourselves, the more accepting we are of others. Conversely, this person needs to "see" others as deficient or less in order to feel better about himself.

We all probably have one or two people in our lives we find difficult. However, this person feels almost everyone is problematic. In reality, it isn't everyone, but it is he who is the problem.

A person with high self-esteem is gentle with his environment, while the arrogant person can often be seen hitting, banging, and forcing inanimate objects to do his will. Just as he tries to do with people, he insists on imposing his "will" onto things and demanding they take heed.

Signs of LE-A

- He's easily frustrated, angry and controlling, feeds off attention and can often be seen as aggressive, not only with people, but his environment as well.

- He has a tendency to overreact to any perceived injustice, no matter how minor.

- He's often bragging and boastful when he has achieved a minor success.

- He's consumed by material possessions, seeking to fortify his sense of importance; no matter what the conversation, he tries to impress the other with his knowledge and is bent on steering the focus back to him.

- He needs to be right, and tries to take control of people and situations, insisting his way is the only way. Also, he's unable to listen to another's point of view, and quickly dismisses their opinions.

- He has highly addictive behavior and may engage in high-risk behavior to "feel alive."

Signs of both LE-D and LE-A*

- He's hyper-sensitive. While the LE-A may become angry or put on a strong front, the LE-D becomes sad and withdrawn.

- He often uses hopeless language and lives in the past, even though it may be largely unpleasant.

- In an unconscious attempt to anchor himself in something definitive, he often paints his world in black and white; unless of course, this does not suit him, in which case he sees shades of gray wherever he needs to.

- He often projects a false image of himself to the rest of the world because he wants others to believe he is something better than he believes himself to be.

- He takes everything personally; what could it be about except him, the center-of-the universe?

- He constantly seeks approval and reassurance from others.

DAVID J. LIEBERMAN

- He's filled with irrational beliefs, has a strong tendency to think emotionally, and uses logic to justify his behavior.

- He is easily frustrated and will shift course, or abandon ship altogether, when the going gets rough.

- He has unhealthy relationships; there are more than a few people in his life whom he simply does not get along well with.

- He blames everyone but himself for his problem and refuses to accept responsibility for much of his life and well-being. He is a perpetual victim.

- He's often depressed or, at a minimum, anxious and uneasy.

- He has difficulty in making decisions. The fear of being wrong often paralyzes him into inaction. He has a strong fear of change in instances where too many variables are out of his control or understanding.

We should note that a person with low self-esteem often cycles between personas of inferiority (the doormat mentality) and superiority (producing arrogance), whereby whichever mode is dominant at a given time yields either negativity directed, inward manifesting hurt and sadness, or outward into anger. By gaging which mode the person is operating in at a given time, you can reasonably predict his overall attitude and behavior

What we have laid out thus far is the complete psychology behind S.N.A.P. With it, you have the ability to better understand the thought and decision-making process, as each profile gives us a very clear window into a person's thinking.

Now, it's simply a matter of plugging the facts into the equation. While Section I offers concrete tactics, Section II is more of an art. In order to get the most out of your new skills, we will now codify the process just a bit, into a specific sequence, so you may more easily adapt the process for various situations and circumstances.

DAVID J. LIEBERMAN

The Art And Science Of Profiling: Real-Life Examples

CHAPTER 15

"Imagination and fiction make up more than three quarters of our real life."

Simone Weil (1909 - 1943)

The two classifications which account for all possible dynamics follow, with real-life examples to illustrate how the system works.

Once you have observed the "colors"—self-esteem, confidence, interest—you put them into the mix to build a fast and complete profile determining thought, feelings, beliefs, and likely behavior. As you will see, some of the colors—even primary and certainly secondary—can have a negligible effect and are not weighted in every calculation. You'll notice that we use the type of interest (not to be confused with the level of interest) as the starting point on which to build our psychological framework. While theoretically you can use any of the colors as a starting point, the type of interest is the easiest to glean, as it is almost always understood by the context of the situation.

Classifications

Class A: a person with no inherent personal interest in the outcome (e.g. jury member, work evaluation, favor for a friend).

Class B: a person with his own obvious interest at heart (e.g. poker, negotiation, sales call).

Note: In instances where a person's level of interest is unknown, such as on a date, apply the techniques in Chapter 5 and then proceed to either formula based on whether or not there is perceived interest.

First, we'll examine situations where the person has no inherent interest and has high self-esteem, then no inherent interest with low self-esteem. Then we'll follow cases where the person has an inherent interest in the outcome and is observed to have high self-esteem, then where he is observed to have low self-esteem.

Class A: A person with no inherent personal interest in the outcome.

Of course a person certainly may want to do the right thing, by having an interest in seeing justice served or in helping out a friend in need. We are speaking, however, about whether or not this person has an inherent desire for a specific outcome benefitting him on a more personal, non-altruistic level.

Recall that self-esteem determines the level of inherent interest in what is at stake, and the greater one's self-esteem, the greater his ability to gain pleasure in pursuing meaningful objectives. With low self-esteem, the value in doing the right thing goes unseen, and one attaches little or no interest in the outcome.

In a situation where the person has no inherent interest, his self-esteem becomes the most influential factor in his thinking and decision-making process. Therefore, this becomes the focus of our initial scan. From there, we begin to draw our profile, and the next section tells what you can conclude from it.

S.N.A.P: General Evaluation

As effort increases, in relation to what is at stake, likelihood of positive or helpful action decreases. However, the higher one's self-esteem, the more resilient is his desire to do what's right over what feels good or looks good. As self-esteem decreases, mood becomes a stronger factor and, even with minimal or no effort, the desire to do what's right weakens. As mood decreases and effort increases, chances of compliance quickly sink fast. With no inherent interest and low self-esteem, whatever is at stake becomes pretty much irrelevant, especially as mood declines.

As mood increases, the person is able to move slightly away from egocentric thinking and can focus, for a time, on another's needs. Therefore, compliance or cooperation is highest when a person with low self-esteem is in a good mood, effort is low, and what is at stake is relatively high. We should add that confidence is rarely a factor when there is no self-interest, as confidence is a function of interest—inversely related. So, with low self-esteem and no inherent interest, the person simply does not care enough to be concerned about his level of effectiveness.

As we know, all low self-esteem is not created equal. An LE-A type person will be less concerned with public perception, while the LE-D type will be more easily swayed by what others may think of his action. While both types are consumed with the opinions of others, LE-A is more interested in satisfying his own needs. If what he wants from the situation looms larger, he will do what is good for him while the LE-D type will more easily accommodate others at his own expense.

Profile When Self-Esteem Is Observed to be High

- Focus shifts to long-term benefit and to others; conscience can override own interests.

- Mood will not ordinarily engage, unless what is at stake is very low.

- Confidence hinges on degree of interest and is not likely to engage, unless interest (in doing what is right, in this case) is extremely high.

The person sees with great intellectual clarity, and emotions are not clouding judgment. Perception is wide and not self-centered. The person is positive and giving, not rude or rushed. He does not need to prove anything, and he is outwardly focused and not at all self-conscious. The person is focused on gathering information to better make a decision and less on how he is coming across. As self-esteem increases further, he will take the higher moral ground, even at his own personal expense.

Profile When Self-Esteem Is Observed to be Low

- Focus shifts to immediate gratification and to self-interests.

- Mood overrides self-esteem.

- Confidence is inversely related to interest, and is unlikely to engage strongly enough to be a factor needing to be weighed.

The Mottos

	Inherent Interest	No Inherent Interest
LE-D	"I'll try."	"I don't want anyone to get mad at me."
LE-A	"I need this."	"Whatever!"
S/E	"I'll do what I can."	"Let's do what is right."

This person sees what he needs to see in order to feel secure and becomes emotionally driven—clouding judgment. He is self-centered and focused on his own needs. He's only out to do what is good for himself, unless he is in a very good mood. The person will be rude and abrupt when he is in a bad mood. So unless there is something in it for him, he will be resistant to cooperation or compromise. The only way to sway him is to appeal to his ego, since his sense of right and wrong is too distorted for appeal to his conscience to be effective.

Real-World Examples

High Self-Esteem Observed

Case A: A prospective juror is being interviewed by a defense attorney for a case in which his client is charged with a serious crime.

Summary: If the defense has good, solid evidence, this juror is a keeper. If the case relies on conjecture, the juror will not easily buy it. However, he's not against feeling sorry for someone and empathizing with his pain. As someone with high self-esteem and no inherent interest, he can easily feel for others. No ego absorbs his attention or interest.

That said, this person is not going to ignore the facts of the case merely because he feels badly for someone. With high self-esteem and no inherent interest in the outcome, the person feels he is right and does not mind sticking to his guns. "I must do what is right. Justice must be served," is his motto, but he will be fair and balanced. He will listen to others but remain firm, unless he has a logical reason to move from his position.

Another factor here is that of beliefs. If a potential juror, for instance, holds a belief that all CEOs are greedy and will do whatever they can to make money, this belief will clearly impact his thinking. Therefore, to eliminate the problem (see Chapter 2, Technique 2), ask correlated questions to see if his thinking is leaning in an unexpected direction.

High Self-Esteem Observed

Case B: A probation officer is preparing a report for the court.

Summary: This scenario is similar to the previous case, with one exception. In this case, a person's job is tied into the situation. So while he doesn't have an inherent personal interest in the outcome, he does have an interest in making good and effective decisions.

Therefore, we must factor in the officer's overall procedure, more heavily weighing his recent decisions. If he's recently made some recommendations that were soft yet well-received, you can expect more to follow. However, the strength of his self-esteem will indicate how far his own belief of right and wrong will deviate from what is "acceptable" in terms of guidelines. We often erroneously conclude that it is the egotist who is willing to "make waves" and march to the beat of his own proverbial drum. This is true only if he has something at stake. Without inherent interest it is the person with a higher degree of self-esteem who is inclined to deviate when it does not personally benefit him or his interests.

Low Self-Esteem Observed

Case A: A prospective juror is being interviewed by a defense attorney for a case in which his client is charged with a serious crime.

Summary: The calculation here is more complicated than it is with his higher self-esteem counterpart. He's naturally preoccupied with himself and doesn't consider the gravity of the case unless he attaches personal meaning. If it's not a high-profile case, the interest level is assumed to be low. He's not likely to weigh facts as much as emotion and is engaged in irrational feelings and subjective thinking.

The egocentric person sees himself in others, so it depends on whom the juror identifies with—the plaintiff or the defendant. He will favor this person. He is thinking, "He is just like me." A strong caveat exists and the attachment can boomerang if the juror feels jealousy toward the one with whom he identifies.

The potential for jealousy is stronger with people similar to us. For instance, a painter is not likely to feel jealous of a surgeon's skill, but another surgeon, particularly one with low self-esteem, identifies more clearly with other doctors, and jealousy is bred. The test is to ask correlated questions (as discussed in Chapter 2) to gauge the way his attachment will fall.

Generally speaking, if he's in a good mood for most of the trial, particularly during deliberation, and the juror identifies with the suspect, he'll lean toward finding the suspect innocent. If he's in a bad mood, he'll favor a guilty verdict. The reason is this: when his mood is bad, his ego fully engages. The unconscious musing is that if other people "like me" are worse off, I must be better off.

The juror (LE-A)can be persuaded if other jurors stroke his ego. But if he becomes enraged, he'll stick to his guns until the very end. If he's had enough and wants to get out, he'll be quicker to acquiesce. His own comfort and needs are of primary importance, over any type of justice. So if the case drags on for a while, then count on his position shifting whenever he feels that he's done.

In contrast, the LE-D person generally has a "herd" mentality; in such cases, he'll statistically agree with the crowd unless he develops a very strong identification with a party. In this case, he'll attempt to "hold his own" until the pressure becomes too unbearable.

Low Self-Esteem Observed

Case B: A probation officer is preparing a report for the court.

Summary: Again, the summary is similar to that of the previous case, except that the person's job is tied into the scenario. Low self-esteem, however, will decrease the person's flexibility. You'll notice a strong tendency to follow a pattern. The strongest indicator of what he will do now is what he has done in the past under similar scenarios. Low self-esteem (LE-A) means he will seek out an identity and want to be known as a certain type of person, such as the "tough, no-nonsense guy." If he deviates from his usual pattern, it will be because he sees the case as very different from others.

Therefore, he doesn't have to change how he sees himself by voting differently than usual. The person is most easily persuaded by showing him how the case is different from the others and allowing him to make a new decision based on new information, as opposed to changing his general thinking about these types of cases.

The LE-D type person is more inclined to again go with the crowd and the prevailing wisdom. He's just as emotional as his LE-A counterpart but more willing to feel for another, as most of his choices revolve around the needs and wants of others over his own. Absent any of these influences, his thinking is similar to the LE-A type.

Class B: A person with his own interests at heart

S.N.A.P: General Evaluation

When self-interest is assumed, a person's level of confidence becomes the dominant influential factor. Because confidence and interest are inversely related, the person's thoughts, feelings, and subsequent actions are based on "how badly he wants "it" versus his perceived chances of being successful.

QUICK TAKE Will a crowd make a difference? Social facilitation is the resulting arousal, when other people are present and our performance can be evaluated. Studies show the arousal enhances our performance on simple tasks but impairs our performance on complex tasks. For instance, when several observers watched below-average players shoot pool, the players made fewer shots. But when the observers watched above-average players shoot pool, the players made more shots. (Michaels, et al.,1982) When you're competing against someone more adept than yourself, do it without others around. However, if you are more competent, have people around to watch, because it will help you to perform better and your opponent worse.

When self-esteem skews high, then *confidence equals action*. Put simply, a person is driven to go after what he wants when he feels good about himself and his chances of success. But because he's acting responsibly, as confidence in his ability to be successful decreases, his desire to put in effort dwindles as well. Therefore, as effort increases, likelihood of action decreases.

Mood is also negligible with higher self-esteem. If what is at stake isn't so important and/or is temporary, mood comes back into play. Doing what's responsible becomes less important because the situation won't have a lasting impact in any significant way.

When self-esteem is on the lower side, mood becomes a stronger factor tied into confidence. As he gets his jolts of emotional fuel from successful encounters, when confidence is high, mood goes with it, and vice-versa. Also, when confidence is high, he'll pursue an objective relentlessly, even more so than someone with high self-esteem. So much so, that even effort (for LE-A) is not much of a factor.

The reason is that his self-worth is wrapped up in actions, not himself. Thus, success will make him like himself more. But for (LE-D), his lack of self-esteem and diminished ego offer little support for making his life better or making him happier. So, he more often gives way to quitting and indulging in immediate gratification to feel good quickly and to distract himself from the opportunity lost. However, for the LE-A, if confidence and mood are low, he becomes angry, frustrated, and easily annoyed. He wants something for himself, and is only interested in himself. Yet, he does not feel good about his chances and is enraged in proportion to his interest level.

Situational Filter

Now we have to factor in something that's not a part of the person's emotional make-up, but a reflection of the situation itself and what is going on in the person's life, which affects his thinking and attitude. It is easy to do the right thing and maintain good values and moral beliefs when there's no self-interest. This statement isn't an indictment of human nature but rather a function of it. The only force holding self-interest in check (when it conflicts with what is right) is self-esteem; and self-esteem is what holds healthy values and beliefs in check.

In some cases, it is quite advantageous, even necessary, to know what is going on in the person's life as it relates to the situation and how it may conflict with his sense of morality. As a person's self-interest increases, it becomes more complicated. The equation is simpler for a person having no inherent self-interest, or even for one who is in an outright competition, because self-interest, while present, does not often indicate a moral dilemma.

This factor can be a wildcard, but you can navigate around it (use the technique in Chapter 3, Sign 2). Briefly, bring up the subject and note if the person becomes more self-conscious. If he does, you are probably nearing the threshold where his values may give way to necessity.

Additionally, when questioning the point at which (if ever) the person's situation will erode his values and beliefs to the level where he will engage in behavior going against his nature, looking for patterns is very helpful. The biggest predictor of future behavior is past behavior. Barring any significant event, or attitude change, you can expect the person to do what he has always done.

If you lure a person away from another firm, you can be sure of one thing: he can be lured away from your firm. Also, a woman finding herself in a relationship with a married man can be sure of one thing: he will, statistically speaking, cheat on her as well.

Profile When Self-Esteem Is Observed to be High

- Focus shifts to long-term benefit.
- Mood is negated, because both self-esteem and interest are up; it comes into play only when the situation is not so important.
- Confidence becomes a strong factor.

This person wants to do what is right, but will reach a point where his moral barometer conflicts with his own interests. For instance, if he finds a wallet with ten dollars and a bunch of credit cards, he is inclined to seek its owner.

However, he is forced into more of an internal struggle should he find a bag of cash filled with hundred-dollar bills. His desire to do what is right and turn it in to the police will, at some point—depending upon his self-esteem and how strong his own needs are—cause him to act against his own moral compass.

Case A: John is in a contract negotiation with you.

Since interest is assumed, the focus now shifts to confidence. If you evaluate his confidence level as high, you're in for a tough battle. High interest, high confidence, and high self-esteem put him into the "zone" where he is pretty much fearless. He's not inclined to make an irrational move, unlike his low-self esteem counterpart. Your surest shot of getting him to budge from his position will be to appeal to his sense of goodness—doing something for you—even though he does not have to comply.

If you note his confidence is low, however, you will more easily gain leverage by raising the possibility that he may walk away with less than he actually expected. Thus, you gain a foothold by tilting his thinking from rational to emotional. Now you have a better chance of his actions deviating from what's in his objective long-term best interest.

Case B: You are playing poker and the hand is down to you and your opponent.

Here, you would use the techniques in Chapter 3 to determine his confidence level and then play accordingly. While you have no way of knowing what his cards are, you can predict the various possible outcomes based upon the following: he will play according to the odds and is not afraid to trust his gut instincts. He is unlikely to make irrational moves or be swayed by emotions. If he does not have a good hand, it will be a calculated bluff, leaning toward risky, but not foolish.

With high confidence noted (adjusting for perception-management), he will tend to play slightly more aggressively, since confidence is linked with mood. Studies show the person is inclined to take more risks if he recently won a big hand or is up overall. If low confidence is noted, his higher self-esteem will generally keep him from deviating from smart play.

Profile When Self-Esteem Is Observed to be Low

- Focus shifts to immediate gratification.
- Mood is factored and may override self-esteem even in situations of objective unimportance, because to a person with low self-esteem, anything can be important if it concerns him and his interests.
- Confidence becomes a strong factor, hinging on interest.

With low self-esteem and high interest, his confidence is easily shaken, and he can appear almost frantic in his dealings as he views this situation as his big chance to turn his life around—his lucky break. With lowered confidence, his perspective is even more skewed, and he is capable of acting completely irrationally and becoming easily angered and frustrated at every roadblock to his brass ring.

Case A: Brad is in a contract negotiation with you.

Low self-esteem and high confidence means he will be highly emotional and reckless; a chance to feel good cannot be ignored. He is hyper-vigilant to every point, and nothing escapes his attention. The negotiation is his opportunity, his time to shine. Expect him to come across larger than life. However, if you note an LE-D tendency, while he is thinking everything we just said, his demeanor will be less than overt and not in-your-face.

With low confidence, he pulls back, scared even when logic dictates staying in the negotiation—he runs. He may also appear completely disinterested; his desires are outside of his reach, and his ego engages to prevent him from being injured. He will now rationalize all of the reasons why it doesn't make sense for him to assert himself. If he has an LE-D type personality, he'll appear dejected; an LE-A may become rude and almost enraged, particularly if interest levels are very high.

Case B: You're playing poker, and the hand is down to you and your opponent.

An LE-A type with high confidence will milk the hand for everything it's worth. His self-worth hangs in the balance of the hand, and his life comes down to this one moment. Any attempt to grandstand, without giving away his hand, will be sought. Note whether he looks around for a witness to his big achievement. An LE-D type is harder to read but is prone to taking note of who is around to witness his success. If his confidence is low, he'll exhibit more withdrawn, less animated behavior.

Working Forward and Backward

Once you get familiar with the process, you can apply your skills in two directions. You'll be able to profile a person and determine thought and behavior patterns, in addition to understanding his emotional make-up in a larger sense. Effective profiling is a two-way street, flowing forward and backward. For example:

You conclude through observation that a tennis player has low self-esteem, high confidence, and high interest. Translation: he gains his sense of self-worth from his abilities. With high interest, he's putting his whole world on the line. Therefore, look at the type of low self-esteem determining his behavior. You can predict that the LE-A will be loud and controlling, possibly smug and annoying.

You know he'll become extremely volatile if things do not go his way. Bad calls will cause him to lash out, and so on. The LE-D person won't even complain over bad calls or become antagonistic, but will portray a somewhat dejected attitude.

You can also work backward. Seeing a person's previous behavior—such as that of our tennis player—can help you surmise that he has low self esteem, high confidence, and high interest.

Look at some examples of how we can predict the outcome or gain insight into the person's emotional makeup if you already know the outcome:

Question: Pam works in the office where her friend was just fired, despite her objection, and replaced by Sue. If you observe Pam has high-self esteem or low self-esteem, what will she do?

Answer: If she has higher esteem, she will choose to do what is right over merely trying to be right. However, if she has lower self-esteem, proving she is right is more important than doing what is best for the office. Therefore, she is likely to behave in an unhelpful way—with behavioral ranges from passive-aggressive to outright sabotaging Sue at her new job.

Question: Kelly, the housekeeper, finds a quarter under the couch and puts it on the table for you to retrieve. Can we say she is honest? What might Kelly do if she finds a crumpled $100 bill in your pants pocket?

Answer: Your odds of getting it back are diminished with Kelly's lower self-esteem. When a person's inherent interest is at stake, we must factor in any situation that may rupture her moral center. The question, "How badly does she need the money?" needs to be put into the equation.

If she has higher self-esteem, only self-interest can move her. So, examine her situation—is she facing eviction or financially strapped? Of course, this assumption isn't absolute. Her morality may hold, but look for signs of erosion.

Question: You want a co-worker to support your project. Will he or won't he?

Answer: As his costs go up, your chances go down. If his support may injure his reputation, the cost of self-interest is weighed against the value of the relationship. Again, self-esteem moves him to do what is right over what looks good (his reputation). A person with an LE-D personality is more inclined to help than an LE-A, as he does not want to risk offending you or making you mad at him.

Question: A woman is on a date and gauging her date's thoughts. She already believes he likes her, but what will he do next?

Answer: The person will be prone to action, if confidence is high. If the confidence level is low, the person will seek image-enhancement. To make himself look better, he'll ask questions and try to engage her. He'll be self-conscious, focusing on himself and how he comes across. It should be noted that he may appear completely disinterested as a defense mechanism to protect against getting his hopes up.

General Profiles

Finally, let's take a look at the six most intriguing and important general profiles. Familiarity will benefit you greatly.

Question: Who is most likely to make a deal or take action?

Answer: High confidence, high interest, high investment, and low self-esteem.

The Logic: The person will be almost frantic in his pursuit. With high confidence, he can't believe his good fortune. Interest is high, so he has motivation. Low self-esteem means he doesn't want to let the opportunity pass by, and high investment means he's already rationalized the worth and doesn't want to further dent his self-image by throwing away his "investment." The type of low self-esteem only comes into play if the person has to assert himself in an uncomfortable situation.

Question: In general, who is most likely to walk away from a deal?

Answer: Low interest, high self-esteem, and low investment.

The Logic: Even with higher interest, he has no emotional pull. Imagine you're the person looking at a home. Even if you like it, it's not the end of the world if you don't get it, so perspective is not skewed. Additionally with this profile and where confidence is low, you can expect with high certainty that he operates with a low level of motivation to take action in this instance.

Question: Who is most easily persuaded?

Answer: Confidence low, interest high.

The Logic: Research shows that in many situations self-esteem cuts both ways in terms of the ability to be persuaded. If you like yourself, you can take a hit to your ego and be wrong. At the same time, you may be more confident in your opinion. With low self-esteem, it's harder to admit you've made an error, but you're also susceptible to tactics of influence and less sure of yourself, overall. Either way, if much has been invested, then being able to influence him along his current course of action is probable, and with less of an investment you are more likely to be effective in swaying him to move in a new direction.

Question: Who's most likely to do the wrong thing (lie, cheat, or steal) or, for that matter, who's most likely to be rigid, stubborn, and inflexible?

Answer: Low self-esteem, high interest, high confidence, and poor mood.

DAVID J. LIEBERMAN

The Logic: This profile produces the absolute worst combination of psychological factors within a given situation. With an inherent high interest and high confidence, he feels he'll be successful in his pursuit and will be relentless. Both types, (LE-A and LE-D) under the right conditions are capable of acting wrongly. In fact, it is not unusual to hear it was "the quiet one who kept to himself" who was responsible for wrongdoing. Of course, the brazen, arrogant person also has the emotional make-up consistent with a high likelihood of this type of behavior.

With a little bit of power, the person becomes a royal pain. Low self-esteem and high confidence produce the lowest probability for cooperation. He feels strong in his position and will define his self-worth on the outcome, since self-esteem is low.

Factor in poor mood, and the psychological dynamic produces extreme irritability and irrational behavior. The person will be stubborn and unyielding, and is ready to pounce in a second on anything over anything. At the same time, his thoughts are highly critical, judgmental, and focused on what you think of him, since his underlying motivation is driven by a search for respect—also a function of self-esteem. So, paradoxically, he will be more argumentative, since he views the world as a competition with his image hanging in the balance.

Question: All things being equal, who's most likely to make a bad choice?

Answer: High interest, low self-esteem.

The Logic: The two factors are most relevant, as both high interest and low self-esteem skew perspective. When we don't see clearly, we can't make good choices. The type of low self-esteem doesn't matter.

Question: Who's most likely to be flexible, honest, and trustworthy?

Answer: High self-esteem, low inherent interest, and good mood.

The Logic: With this profile, the person is clearly willing to be flexible. High self-esteem means he doesn't need to hold on to a position, since his ego doesn't mind bending as long as it doesn't conflict with his sense of morality. Low inherent interest means he doesn't care personally, and a good mood means he will likely move into a giving mode.

S.N.A.P provides a terrific edge in almost any situation. It allows you to gain a high level of insight into a person's thinking and psyche without having to spend much time with the person that you wish to profile. Of course, as we've illustrated, profiling, while systematic, is not exempt from ambiguity and miscues.

Once you become more familiar, however, with what to look for and what to listen to, your ability to read a person will become almost instinctual.

DAVID J. LIEBERMAN

Conclusion

Dear Reader:

The techniques in Section I allow you a great deal of insight into people, and will help you gain the advantage in about every situation. Once you've mastered the process in Section II, it will become second nature. When it does, you'll possess one of the most important, valuable tools available to help you in all areas of your life.

It is my fondest hope that this book will help you to better accomplish your worthwhile goals and objectives in life. Indeed, knowing if you are being taken advantage of, lied to, or manipulated will save you from unnecessary emotional, financial, and possible physical hardship. Perhaps, after reading this book and implementing its strategies, you will have gained a better understanding of human nature. As a result, you'll have more insight into yourself, which will help you to be a better, healthier person and to enjoy richer and more meaningful relationships.

I wish you a good life and good relationships.

Warmest wishes,
David

Bibliography

Adams, S. FBI Bulletin. (1994). *Statement analysis: what do suspects' words really reveal?*

Asch, S. E. (1956). Studies of independence and conformity: A minority of one against a unanimous majority. *Psychological monographs*, 70.

Ekman, P. (1985). Telling lies: Clues to deceit in the marketplace, marriage, and politics. New York: Norton.

Caro, Mike. (2003). *Caro's book of poker tells.* New York, NY: Cardoza Publishing.

De Becker, Gavin. (1997). *The Gift of Fear.* New York, NY: Dell Publishing.

Dichter, Ernest. (1964). *Handbook of consumer motivations: The psychology of the world of objects.* New York, NY: McGraw Hill.

Gorn, Gerald. (1982). The effects of music, in advertising, on choice behavior: A classical conditioning approach. *Journal of Marketing*, 46(1), 94-101.

Freedman, J. L., Cunningham, J. A., & Krismer, K. (1992). Inferred values and the reverse-incentive effect in induced compliance. *Journal of Personality and Social Psychology*, 62, 357-368.

Freedman, J. L., & Fraser, S. C. (1996). Compliance without pressure: The foot-in-the-door technique. *Journal of Personality and Social Psychology, 4.*

Friedman, B. (2000, January). Designing casinos to dominate the competition: The Friedman International standards of casino design. *Institute for the Study of Gambling and Commercial Gaming.*

Hare, R. D. (1999) Without conscience: *The disturbing world of the psychopaths among us.* New York, NY: Guilford Press.

Lewicki, P. (1985). Nonconscious biasing effects of single instances on subsequent judgements. *Journal of Personality and Social Psychology*, 48, 563-574.

Lieberman, D. J. (1998). *Never be lied to again.* New York, NY: St. Martin's.

Lieberman, D. J. (2000). *Get anyone to do anything.* New York, NY: St. Martin's.

Lubow, R. E. & Fein, O. (1996). Pupillary size in response to a visual guilty knowledge test: New technique for the detection of deception. *Journal of Experimental Psychology: Applied*, 2(2), 164-177.

about the author

David J. Lieberman, Ph.D., is an award-winning author and internationally recognized leader in the field of human behavior and interpersonal relationships.

Techniques based on his six books, which have been translated into 18 languages and include two New York Times bestsellers, are used by the FBI, The Department of the Navy, Fortune 500 companies, and by governments and corporations in more than 25 countries.

Dr. Lieberman has appeared as a guest expert on more than 200 programs such as The Today Show, Fox News, PBS, and The View, and his work has been featured in publications around the world.

Dr. Lieberman, whose Ph.D. is in psychology, lectures and holds workshops across the country on a variety of topics. He lives in New Jersey.

Contact:
Dr. David J. Liebeman   Email DJLMedia@aol.com
c/o Viter Press   Fax 772-619-7828
1072 Madison Ave.
Lakewood, NJ 08701